Top 25 locator map
(continues on inside
back cover)
◀

CityPack
Bangkok

**ANTHONY SATTIN AND
SYLVIE FRANQUET**

If you have any comments
or suggestions for this guide
you can contact the editor at
Citypack@theAA.com

AA Publishing
Find out more about AA Publishing and the wide range
of travel publications and services the AA provides by
visiting our website at www.theAA.com/bookshop

About This Book

KEY TO SYMBOLS

➕ Map reference to the accompanying fold-out map and Top 25 locator map

✉ Address

☎ Telephone number

🕐 Opening/closing times

🍴 Restaurant or café on premises or nearby

🚆 Nearest railway station

Ⓢ Nearest subway (tube) station

🚌 Nearest bus route

🚢 Nearest riverboat or ferry stop

♿ Facilities for visitors with disabilities

✋ Admission charges: Expensive (over 200B), Moderate (100–200B) and Inexpensive (less than 100B).

↔ Other nearby places of interest

❓ Other practical information

▶ Indicates the page where you will find a fuller description

ℹ Tourist information

ORGANIZATION

This guide is divided into six chapters:

- Planning Ahead, Getting There
- Living Bangkok—Bangkok Now, Bangkok Then, Time to Shop, Out and About, Walks, Bangkok by Night
- Bangkok's Top 25 Sights
- Bangkok's Best—best of the rest
- Where To—detailed listings of restaurants, hotels, shops and nightlife
- Travel Facts—practical information

In addition, easy-to-read side panels provide extra facts and snippets, highlights of places to visit and invaluable practical advice.

The colors of the tabs on the page corners match the colors of the triangles aligned with the chapter names on the contents page opposite.

MAPS

The fold-out map in the wallet at the back of this book is a comprehensive street plan of Bangkok. The first (or only) grid reference given for each attraction refers to this map. **The Top 25 locator map** found on the inside front and back covers of the book itself is for quick reference. It shows the Top 25 Sights, described on pages 26–50, which are clearly plotted by number (**1**–**25**, not page number) across the city. The second map reference given for the Top 25 Sights refers to this map.

Contents

Planning Ahead

WHEN TO GO

The most pleasant time to visit, and the peak tourist season, is from November to early March, so flights and lodgings are best reserved ahead. During the hot season, invest in an air-conditioned room. In the rainy season, peaking in September to October, it's wettest at dusk. Frequent floods at this time bring traffic to a standstill.

TIME

Bangkok is 12 hours ahead of EST. In winter: UK is 7 hours behind, Europe 6 hours, New York 12 hours, Australia 3 hours. In summer: add 1 hour.

AVERAGE DAILY MAXIMUM TEMPERATURES

JAN	FEB	MAR	APR	MAY	JUN	JUL	AUG	SEP	OCT	NOV	DEC
83°F	83°F	85°F	86°F	87°F	87°F	86°F	87°F	87°F	86°F	85°F	83°F
28°C	28°C	29°C	30°C	31°C	31°C	30°C	31°C	31°C	30°C	29°C	28°C

Bangkok has three distinct seasons:

Hot season (March to May)—The climate can be unbearable because the high temperatures are intensified by the 90 percent humidity.
Rainy season (June to October)—Hot and humid days are followed by rain, usually at dusk.
Cool season (November to February)—The sky is usually bright and clear; days are reasonably cool and nights pleasantly warm.

WHAT'S ON

January *Bangkok nternational Film Festival*: With over 150 films from around the world.
February *Chinese New Year* (early Feb): Temples busy, shops close.
Maga Puja: Candle-lit processions at *wats* for full moon.
March *Kite fights and festivals*: (late Feb–Apr): on Sanam Luang.
Chakri Day (6 Apr): Celebrates the founding in 1782 of the Chakri dynasty.
Songkran (12–14 Apr): The Thai New Year.

May *Royal Plowing Ceremony* (early May): Start of the rice-planting season: on Sanam Luang.
Visaka Puja (mid-May): Celebrates the birth, enlightenment and death of the Buddha.
July *Asalha Puja*: Marks Buddha's first sermon and the start of a three-month Rains Retreat.
August *HM Queen Sirikit's Birthday* (12 Aug).
September *Moon Festival*: The Chinese community honors the moon goddess.
October *Ok Pansa*: End of

the three-month Rains Retreat. Monks are presented with new robes and gifts.
Royal Barge Ceremony: The king takes a fleet of spectacular barges to Wat Arun to present new robes to the monks. Not annual.
November *Loy Krathong* (Nov full moon): Small banana-leaf boats with flowers and candles float in honor of water spirits.
Long-boat races
December *Trooping the Color* (3 Dec): Starts a week celebrating the King's birthday (5 Dec).

BANGKOK ONLINE

www.tourismthailand.org
Official site of the Tourism Authority of Thailand with a range of information on Thai art, culture and food, as well as practical information, links to official websites and listings.

www.bkkmetro.com
The on-line version of the popular magazine *Metro*, with all the latest on trendy bars, exhibitions and new restaurants and shops.

www.bangkoksite.com
Useful information about Bangkok's main sights with plenty of pictures as well as listings for events, bars and restaurants.

www.bangkokpost.net
On-line offering of the daily Bangkok Post with new items, economic reviews, weather reports, restaurant reviews, and articles on the capital's sights, culture and art.

www.bangkok.com
Comprehensive guide to the city's temples, museums, markets, great shopping and exotic nightlife, as well as tips to make the most of your stay.

www.into-asia.com
Easy-to-use site that gives a general insight into Thai language and culture as well as possible good and bad impressions when you first arrive in Bangkok. Useful advice about scams and tourist traps.

www.khaosanroad.com
The best website for budget travelers, staying around Khaosan Road, with listings, reviews of new bars, cheap deals and even job offers.

www.bangkok.thailandtoday.com
Useful site for those staying in or visiting Rattanakosin and the Banglamphu areas, with sights, shopping, accommodations, restaurants, walks and dinner cruises.

GOOD TRAVEL SITES

www.fodors.com
A complete travel-planning site. You can research prices and weather; reserve air tickets, cars and rooms; ask questions (and get answers) from fellow travelers.

www.bangkok-hotels-network.com
A quick finder for hotels for all budgets at discounted prices—sometimes up to 75 percent—as well as special deals and packages.

CYBERCAFÉS

You'll find hundreds of cybercafés all over the city. Most charge between 1 and 5B a mintue but the cheaper ones have slower connections.

Patpont Internet
➕ G11 ✉ Patpong Soi 2, off Thanon Surawong
🕐 Daily 1pm–4am
💷 1B per minute

Coffee World
➕ J9 ✉ Between Sois 3 and 5, Thanon Sukhumwit
☎ 02-252 0253
🕐 8am–10pm
💷 100B for 80 minutes

Getting There

ENTRY REQUIREMENTS

You must hold a valid passport and proof of onward passage. Nationals of the UK, US, Ireland, Australia, Canada, New Zealand and most European countries holding a passport valid for six months and proof of return or onward passage can stay for 30 days without a visa.

ARRIVING

All major airlines have direct flights into Bangkok. The international airport is in Don Muang, 16 miles (25km) north of the city center. There are two international terminals, and one domestic from where Thai Airlines, the national carrier, operates internal flights.

MONEY

The currency is the Baht (B), divided in 100 satang. The coins are 25 and 50 satang, 1 Baht, 5 Baht and 10 Baht. Notes are 10, 20, 50, 100, 500 and 1,000 Baht.

50 Baht

100 Baht

500 Baht

1000 Baht

ARRIVING BY AIR

A walkway connects Terminal 1 with Don Muang train station, from where trains run more or less every 15 minutes between 5am–8pm to Hualamphong Station (30B, 1 hour). An air-conditioned bus service running every 15 minutes 5.30am–12.30am goes to Thanon Silom (100B, 45 minutes), Sukhumvit (100B, 35 minutes) and Banghlampu (100B, 60 minutes). Minivans and limousines (500–700B) can be booked and prepaid at the Thai Airways Limousine desk, counter 7, which also issues tickets for the Airport Express Train.

Use only metered public taxis from the stand outside the airport; ignore the taxi touts in the terminal. You pay the fare on the meter plus 50B extra for waiting in line and 50B for the expressway on top of the meter fare (takes 20–45 minutes into town, total cost around 400B). Always remind the driver to switch on the meter.

ARRIVING BY TRAIN

Malaysia and Singapore trains arrive at Hualamphong Station in the city center. Regular buses can take you on to your destination.

GETTING AROUND

The elevated **BTS Skytrain** (☎ 0 2275 7612 www.bts.co.th) is by far the fastest, coolest and most comfortable way to get around. Trains run every few minutes from 6am–midnight at 10–40B a trip. There are two lines and neither serves the old city. The only change between lines is at Siam Central Station. Free shuttle buses connect with the Skytrain on certain routes. The recently opened **Subway** (**MRTA** ☎ 0 2246 5733; www.mrta.co.th) operates the 12-mile (20km-long) **Blue Line** from Hualamphong station to Bang Sue. There are 21 stations including four that link up with the Skytrain. An extension is already planned on this line, as well two new lines (orange and purple). Fares are 15B to 40B, depending on the distance traveled.

The best way to see the old city is to take the Skytrain to Saphan Taksin and connect with the **Chao Phraya River Express Boats**, which serve piers (*tha*), marked on the fold-out map, on both sides of the river. They avoid traffic and are fast, enjoyable and inexpensive (5–10B). Boats run about every 10 minutes daily 6–6. Alongside express boat piers are piers for smaller cross-river ferries. Long-tail boats (5–10B) leave for Thonburi from Ratchawong, Tian, Chang Wang Luang and Maha Rat.

Public buses are inexpensive but very crowded and popular with pickpockets. They can also be hot and sticky, and it may be worth paying for an air-conditioned public bus (indicated as *A/C bus* in this guide). Service stops at 11pm, although a few night buses run, including the No. 2 to Thanon Sukhumwit from Sanam Luang. Red air-conditioned Microbuses cost 30B.

Taxis are usually air-conditioned and metered—check it's switched on. The flagfare is 35B. A 24-hour phone-a-cab service charges 20B over the metered fare (☎ 0 2377 1771). Motorbike taxis are cheaper and faster, but can be dangerous. Tuktuks, the motorized open-front three-wheelers, should only be used for short distances owing to pollution. Agree a price in advance.

INSURANCE

Check your policy and buy any necessary supplements. It is vital that travel insurance covers medical expenses, in addition to accident, trip cancellation, baggage loss and theft. Check the policy covers any continuing treatment for a chronic condition. Keep all your receipts in case you need to make a claim.

WHERE TO GET MAPS

The best map to Bangkok is Nancy Chandler's Map of Bangkok available from most English-language bookshops in the city.

VISITORS WITH DISABILITIES

Bangkok is particularly difficult for visitors with disabilities–sidewalks are uneven, streets busy with traffic and the river boats hardly stop long enough for anyone to jump on. For information call Disabled People's International ☎ 0 2583 3021 or the Association of Physically Handicapped in Thailand ☎ 0 2951 0569.

Living
Bangkok

Bangkok Now

Musicians playing classical Thai music

Bangkok is undoubtedly exotic but can also be elusive. Many visitors will stop there briefly en route to somewhere else and visit the main sights without digging a little deeper under the surface. Those who do make the effort may find the ever-smiling Thais inscrutable, partly because, as the only country in Southeast Asia

NEIGHBORHOODS

• Rattanakosin (Royal Island), where Bangkok began in 1782, is the city's spiritual heart with its main sights: the Grand Palace and the Temple of the Emerald Buddha. Nearby, the Chao Phraya River is one of the pleasantest places in the city and is a delightful thoroughfare. Farther south is the busy district of Chinatown and across the river is Thonburi, which despite appearances, remains very traditional. Rama V moved the palace away from the river to Dusit, now a quiet residential neighborhood north of Rattanakosin. The financial heart of the city is around Sathorn and Silom Road, with some of the most beautiful skyscrapers in town. The most modern part of the city is around Thanon Sukhumvit, one of its longest roads, with most of the shopping centers, restaurants and nightlife.

A MONK'S DAY

● Monks wake early. Up before dawn, they recite morning prayers before leaving on their rounds of the neighborhood with their alms bowls, into which people put food offerings. The monks rely entirely on the generosity of the community for their livelihood. The life of a monk is guided by 227 moral precepts, and should be one of retreat and contemplation.

Locally harvested fruit and vegetables piled onto the open deck of a Chinese trader's boat at a Bangkok floating market

that was never colonized, Thailand has a unique identity that can be hard to understand.

If first impressions were lasting, few people would return to Bangkok. "The City of Angels" also nicknamed the "Big Mango" is now a very big mango indeed. The view from the road in from the airport is not quite the anticipated skyline of exotic temples, *chedis* and palm trees. That is how it used to be, but today you will see skyscrapers and concrete in all directions. Like any modern city, the roads underneath the expressway are jammed with traffic at any time of day, and even in early morning the air is fogged with pollution. However the many pleasures and delights of Bangkok are there to be found and because they are sometimes hidden, they seem even sweeter. Those who find them often fall in love with the city forever.

Bangkok has experienced the full urban development cycle in two dramatic centuries, growing beyond its origins by the Chao Phraya River (► 16–17). The last three decades in particular saw an amazing building boom when contractors worked round the clock to meet the demand

Above: *Worshippers at Erawan Shrine*
Center: *River taxi*

MAI PEN RAI

• This expression, (which translates roughly as "never mind," "no problem," "it doesn't matter) goes together with *jai yen* (literally "cool heart"), the social imperative that one should not show one's feelings openly. So even if something bothers people, they'll say "mai pen rai." What they think is another matter.

for new property. Bangkok has leaped into the future and the dynamic process is thrilling and exciting. Sometimes no problem seems too great: Some of the world's worst traffic snarl-ups have been solved by a network of expressways, the super efficient Skytrain and the new Subway opened during the summer of 2004. Meanwhile, the move away from the waterfront, initiated by Rama V when he traveled between the palace and Dusit from 1900 onward, has turned full circle. Now, those who can afford it are returning to live and work by the river, with its fresher air, cooling breezes and improving transport.

There is nostalgia for the sight of old Siam, where only the temple roofs stood out above the wooden houses on stilts, and where people moved around with boats on the *klongs* (canals). Yet some elements of old Bangkok have survived the onslaught of modernity. The city's old teak houses are undergoing restoration and preservation (▶ 56). A trip by boat into the *klongs* or to Nonthaburi (▶ 60) reveals that many people still live a very traditional life on or near the water. Even from the elevated Skytrain you can pick out many vintage residential

Erawan Shrine dancers

structures buried in lush tropical gardens, and detect the outline of beautiful *wats* (temples) dwarfed by the tower blocks. The markets (➤ 54–55), where most residents still prefer to shop, are as seemingly chaotic but as colorful, fascinating and exotic as ever.

Beyond these outward signs, although the city's inhabitants appear to favor all things western and new, they remain spiritual and conservative at heart. Fashionable young girls in designer clothes still bring offerings to Erawan Shrine

---

LONG LIVE THE KING

● The national anthem is still played at Hualampong Station, before movies and on television at 8am and 6pm daily. This is not mere lip service: HM King Bhumibol Adulyadej (Rama IX), the world's longest-reigning monarch, is adored in a way that puzzles many foreigners. The king's position of "revered worship" is assured by the constitution, but he has earned esteem for his public projects and his able leadership (he defused the explosive situation after the 1992 anti-government protests in Bangkok).

FASHION CAPITAL

● Bangkok was the capital of fake designer gear—Cartier watches and Versace T-shirts—but in recent years some excellent young Thai designers are doing their own collections. Their work can be seen in shops around Siam Square and at the Emporium Shopping Complex (➤ 76). The Thai government has established its Bangkok Fashion City project to promote Bangkok as a world-class fashion and design hub by 2005.

13

Above: *The lobby of Bangkok's Oriental Hotel*
Center: *Changing of the Guard at the Grand Palace*
Right: *Wat Pho reclining Buddha*

(▶ 46), while young Thais on the Skytrain fold their hands together in a *wai* (salutation) when they pass a temple or a shrine. A visit to a temple reveals this deep-seated religiousness, particularly during one of the many Buddhist festivals. A similar attitude is shown to the king and the royal family. Thai law forbids public criticism of them, but it seems that Thais generally admire their ruler, and he remains a moral guide at a time when political leaders are seen as corrupt.

Sanuk, an essential part of Thai culture, is generally translated as fun or pleasure, but it means a lot more than that. For Thais, life is divided into activities that are *sanuk*, and others that are not, which means they are the worst possible thing. Hobbies, sports and other leisure activities are

---

RED-HOT CHILLIS

● The Portuguese—the first Europeans to trade with Ayutthaya (as Thailand was originally known)—brought chillis from South America in the 16th century. Thai cuisine now uses over forty varieties of chillis (*prik* in Thai), from the long and mild to the tiny and deadly hot.

obviously *sanuk*, but more importantly, Thais believe that work—even hard work—should be *sanuk* as well, which for Thais means that it should not be a routine or solitary occupation. Accordingly Thais try to have fun while they work and have even more fun afterwards. Bangkok is often considered as Thailand's center of *sanuk*. Good food is definitely *sanuk*, and everywhere you look, from the busy restaurants to the thousands of street stalls, and at any time of the day, people always seem to be eating.

Shopping is perhaps the ultimate *sanuk*, as open-fronted stalls seem to line every street and a new shopping mall seems to pop up monthly. And to cope with so much *sanuk*, Bangkok residents and travelers alike seek out spas (► 58-59), the latest rage—hideaways where you can shake off urban stress and be pampered in all the delights of the East.

Another essential factor in Thai society is the concept of *sabai*, translated as contentment or well-being. In the best of all circumstances, life will be both *sanuk* and *sabai*—then indeed the Thais consider themselves well off.

FACTS AND FIGURES

• Roughly 10 percent of all Thais (6.5 million people) live in Bangkok, with a further 1.4 million in its satellite cities.

• Nearly 80 percent of Thai university graduates live in Bangkok.

• Bangkok's first paved road, Thanon Charoen Krung, or New Road, was laid in 1862.

• Thais have 13 different words for "smile."

• Literacy stands at 96 percent and all Thais are entitled to 12 years of free education.

15

Bangkok Then

Above: *King Chulalongkorn*
(Rama V)
Above Right: *Queen Sirikit*

THE NEW CAPITAL

In 1768, after the Burmese destroyed Ayutthaya, the previous Thai capital, General Phraya Taksin established a new capital at Thonburi, where he was crowned King Boromaraja IV (commonly known as King Taksin). As the Burmese were dragged into a conflict with China, Taksin built an empire that included Lanna (northern Thailand), Cambodia and parts of Laos.

In 1782 Taksin was deposed by one of his generals, Thong Duang (the man responsible for bringing the Emerald Buddha back from Laos), who was crowned Rama I. He built a new capital, which he called Krung Thep ("City of Angels"); today the city is known as Bangkok.

1530s King Phrajai (ruled 1534–46) re-routes the Chao Phraya river some 47 miles (76km) south of his capital Ayutthaya (► 20), creating Thonburi on the west bank and Bang Makok on the east.

1825 King Rama III (ruled 1824–51) responds to growing European influence by closing the mouth of the Chao Phraya river with a massive iron chain. His isolationist policy fails to work: The Burney Treaty of 1826 lowers taxes on British goods passing through Bangkok in return for guarantees of Thai sovereignty.

1851 Unlike his brother, King Rama IV (ruled 1851–68) encourages change. His vision and political skills ensure that Thailand is the only state in the region to retain independence during the colonial period.

1868 Rama V (King Chulalongkorn, ruled 1868–1910) continues social reforms, builds railways, has electricity installed in Bangkok (1884) and encourages closer contacts with the West, but is forced to cede territory in Indo-China.

1932 King Prajadhipok (Rama VII, ruled 1925–35) celebrates the 150th anniversary of the Chakri Dynasty in

April, but in the same year a bloodless coup replaces absolute monarchy with a constitutional monarchy. The king abdicates in 1935.

1939 The country's name is changed from Siam to Prathet Thai, meaning "Land of the Thais."

1946 Thailand is admitted to the United Nations. King Rama VIII, who has spent most of his life in Europe, arrives in Thailand but dies in a tragic shooting incident soon after. He is succeeded by his brother, the still-reigning HM King Bhumibol Adulyadej (King Rama IX).

1947– Several military coups challenge the
1992 democratically elected government.

1992 Democracy is restored following the intervention of King Bhumibol.

1997 The economy crashes. The baht is devalued.

1998– The International Monetary Fund
2000 implements an economic rescue package.

2004 Thais are very disenchanted with their government over midnight closing times for the entertainment business, and government decides to extend them until 1am.

Above: *Streets are lit up for the King's birthday*
Above left: *The vast colonial-style National Assembly, which before the 1932 coup was the Marble Throne Hall*
Above far left: *Detail of the Lak Muang Shrine, erected in 1782 by Rama I and rebuilt under Rama VI*

WEST MEETS EAST

In the 1960s, the US began building military bases within Thailand to help with the Vietnam War. The needs of the US military brought huge sums of money into Thailand and helped transform Bangkok into the burgeoning modern city it is today.

17

Time to Shop

Below: *Silk for sale at Patpong Market*
Below center: *Roses at Chatuchak Market*

It's hard to resist bargains. Traditional markets are chockablock with exotic produce and other food items as well as well-made handicrafts. The ultra-smart shopping centers stock the latest from

HARD BARGAIN

Although prices are fixed in department stores, bargaining is very much a part of life elsewhere, so ask for a good discount where prices are not marked. In bargaining stick to these basic rules:
Bargain only if you intend to buy.
Before buying in street markets, get an idea of prices elsewhere.
Always let the vendor give you a price first, then offer a lower price.
Don't get stuck over a few baht–it's a waste of time for everyone.

Prada or Louis Vuitton outfits (albeit only in tiny Asian sizes). If you don't find the clothes, shoes or furniture you want, you can have it made within a few days.

Fabrics are a good buy. Thai silk comes in several weights and a variety of rich and subtle colors and patterns. HM Queen Sirikit has made great efforts to promote Mudmee, the tie-dyed silk produced in Northeastern Thailand. The Phahurat area is lined with shops selling Indian silks and synthetics, while cotton fabrics, beautiful batiks, often worn as sarongs, and traditional Thai cotton clothing are sold at the Chatuchak Weekend Market (▶ 48) and on Khao San Road.

Good crafts, locally made or imported from neighboring Laos, Cambodia or Burma, come in a great selection at specialist shops and markets. The inexpensive triangular pillows (*mawn khaan*) make great gifts, although they are heavy and bulky to carry back. Benjarong, traditional royal Thai porcelain, is covered in brightly glazed enamel and used as food containers or serving dishes. You can buy simple but fine celadon, glazed pottery that comes in jade green, purple,

Above: *Apples for sale*
Left: *Florist at Chatuchak Market*

blue and brown. Nielloware, silver objects inlaid with niello, and bronze and hand-beaten brassware are other good buys.

Although fine antiques from all over the region are available in Bangkok, don't expect bargains. The best and priciest objects are on the third and fourth floors of the River City Shopping Center; better value can be found at the Chatuchak Weekend Market (► 48). Reputable shops will help you get the necessary export permit for most antiques. Otherwise you must apply for a licence from Fine Arts (☎ 0 2226 1661).

Jewelry and cut or uncut gems, particularly blue sapphires and rubies, are excellent value. You need to know what you are buying—sometimes colored glass is passed off as gems. Reputable jewelers belong to "The Jewel Fest Club" and will issue a certificate of authenticity and a guarantee to refund (less 10 percent) if goods are returned within 30 days. Always pay with a credit card.

SHOPPING DISTRICTS

Sukhumwit Soi 23 has excellent craft shops including Rasi Sayam. Phahurat is known for its fabric stores. Silom Road has tourist-oriented shops, and Patpong night market is famous for its fakes. Many Thai designers have stores near Siam Square and at the Emporium Shopping Complex (► 76). The Khao San area in Banglamphu is good for cheap clothes, bootleg CDs and silverware. The best all round place to buy crafts, antiques and clothes is the Chatuchak Weekend Market (► 48).

19

Out and About

MORE IDEAS

East West Siam (☎ 0 2651 9101; fax 0 2651 9766; www.east-west-siam.com) runs unusual canal tours through more remote Thonburi canals with visits to a traditional Thai teak house for lunch and a cooking lesson, a small temple and a primary school.

Several companies offer night cruises with Thai food and Thai classical dance (➤ 83). The Oriental Hotel (➤ 41), runs an afternoon Thai Culture Programme ☒ 48 Soi Oriental ☎ 0 2659 9000. After an introduction to Thai ways. there's a canal trip (Monday), a class on Thai religion with a visit to Wat Po (Tuesday) and Thai art with a visit to the National Museum (Friday).

Amazing Bangkok Cyclists runs daily cycling tours through backstreets and among houses on stilts and paddy fields (☎ 0 2712 9301; www.realasia.net).

Above: Wat Yai Chai Mongkol in Ayutthaya
Above right: JEATH Museum interior

ORGANIZED SIGHTSEEING

The Bangkok Tourist Bureau (☒ 17/1 Thanon Phra Athit, Pra Nakhon ☎ 0 2225 7612; www. bangkoktourist.bma.go.th) organizes cycle tours around Rattanakosin and Thonburi, as well as canal tours on little-visited *klongs* (canals) and

cultural walks around the city. Here you can also pick up maps, information about excursions, and a list of accredited travel agents. Tour operators are on many street corners in Bangkok, and most hotels have a counter that offers excursions.

BTS Skytrain together with Chao Phraya Express Boat run guided tours of Bangkok's main sights (☎ 0 2623 6001). Boat Co. Ltd. (☎ 0 2412 0207) is a small company running daily river and canal tours each afternoon from the River City Shopping Complex pier.

EXCURSIONS
AYUTTHAYA, BANG PA-IN AND BANG SAI

When Bangkok was a small village, Ayutthaya was Thailand's capital, a glittering city on an artificial island encircled by canals, with scores of palaces, temples and over a million inhabitants. For over 400 years, until 1767 when it was sacked by the Burmese, the old city has been designated a World Heritage Site by UNESCO and to get an overview of the scattered remains start off at the Historical Study Center (Thanon Rotchana ☎ 0 3524 5124). The temples of Wat Mahathat, Wat Ratburana and Viharn Phra

Mongkol Bopit are not to be missed. In the mid-19th century at nearby Bang Pa-In, the Thai royal family built a retreat incorporating classical Thai, Chinese and Italian architecture. At Bang Sai, HM Queen Sirikit helped establish a foundation for crafts, where handiworks are for sale.

RIVER KWAI

The focus of David Lean's movie *The Bridge on the River Kwai*, the Death Railway across this river was built by Allied prisoners of war and Asian laborers in the 1940s with the loss of many lives, then rebuilt after the war. A tourist train now runs along the tracks. Kanchanaburi, the town near the bridge, is the site of the JEATH War Museum and the Kanchanaburi War Cemetery, the last resting place of 6,982 Allied prisoners of war. The Chung Kai War Cemetery contains the graves of 1,750 of the estimated 16,000 Allied prisoners of war who died during construction of the railway.

MUANG BORAN (ANCIENT CITY)

This large open-air museum—where more than 100 tiny versions of the most important Thai temples, palaces and traditional houses are spread over a Thailand-shaped area—could be tacky. But is actually well done and makes for a pleasant day out. Heat permitting, the lush tropical gardens are great for cycling and, since this is Thailand, food stalls and restaurants offer plenty of opportunities for snacks and drink.

INFORMATION

AYUTTHAYA
Distance 46 miles (76km)
Journey Time 1½–2hours
🚆 Half hourly trains (journey time 1½ hours) from Hua Lamphong (6.20–9.30am, 6–10pm)
🚌 Hourly buses (takes 2 hours) from Northern Bus Terminal Mo Chit
🛈 TAT Office ✉ Thanon Si Sanphet ☎ 0 3524 6076
Boat tours with Chao Phraya Chartered (► 20) or plus Oriental Queen (☎ 0 2236 0400) and other companies

RIVER KWAI
Distance 79 miles (130km) from Bangkok
Journey Time 3 hours
🚆 Two trains daily for Kanchanaburi from Bangkok Noi Railway Station
🚌 Buses from Bangkok's Southern Bus Terminal, Thonburi (every 20 minutes until 7pm). Minibuses from Thanon Khao San guesthouses 🛈 TAT office ✉ Thanon Saengchuto, near the bus terminal ☎ 0 3451 1200

MUANG BORAN
Distance 20 miles (33km)
Journey Time 2 hours
🕐 Daily 8am–5pm
🍴 Cheap. Cycle rental 50B
🚌 A/C bus 507, 508, 511 from On Nut Skytrain station to Samut Prakan, then minibus 36, 6B

Walks

RATTANAKOSIN (ROYAL CITY)

See where it all began, with the grandest of the city's temples, street markets, a park and, perhaps, a relaxing massage on the way.

Start at Maha Rat pier, turning right on Thanon Maha Rat and immediately left on Drok Sillapakorn. The entrance to one of Bangkok's oldest temple complexes, Wat Mahathat, is on the left, opposite Sanam Luang. Walk across Sanam Luang to the city's shrine, the Lak Muang pillar, more or less opposite the entrance to the Grand Palace. Veer to the right onto Thanon Nophralan and make a left turn on Thanon Maha Rat to stroll through the thriving street markets that sell amulets, fruits and various portraits of the king. Past the palace, on the left-hand side, rise the impressive roofs and *chedis* (pagodas) of Wat Po, where you can relax with a massage (➤ 35, 59).

Walk along Thanon Chethuphon, take a left on busy Thanon Sanam Chai, then turn right onto Thanon Sararom. Wat Ratchapradit is on the right and a bizarre sculpture of a pig lies at the end of the street. Cross the canal by the footbridge to Thanon Ratchabopit, with yet

Wat Suthat was built in early-Bangkok style. It is surrounded by Chinese pagodas

another temple, Wat Ratchabopit, to the right. Continue along the same street and make a left turn on Thanon Titong, with its local shops. At the intersection with Thanon Bamrung Muang, explore the wonderful Wat Suthat and the nearby Giant Swing. Head along Thanon Din So toward Democracy Monument, built in honor of the modern Thai parliamentary monarchy and now a chaotic traffic circle.

For refreshments try the food and drink stalls on Sanam Luang and near Wat Po. There are several small restaurants on Thanon Nophralan, opposite the entrance to the Grand Palace, serving good international and Thai food as well as ice cream.

A stallholder skilfully tosses noodles at a street side Chinese food stall

THE NARROW LANES OF CHINATOWN

From Ratchawong pier, walk along Thanon Ratchawong and then turn left onto Thanon Annuwong. To the right is an old Chinese house. Walk on as far as Thanon Maha Chak. Take a right here and walk for 160 yards (150m) until you see an ornate portal on the left leading to Wat Chakrawat; visit the crocodile pond.

Return to Thanon Maha Chak and turn left, continuing as far as busy Soi Wanit 1 (Sampeng Lane). Turn right here, cross over Thanon Ratchawong, and carry straight on, exploring the alleys but always returning to Sampeng Lane as it is easy to get lost. At No. 360, turn left into Soi 16, with its amazing variety of food products. Cross Thanon Yaowarat and walk to Thanon Charoen Krung. Cross the road and continue about 30 yards (30m) to the left, past fruit and sweet stalls, to the entrance of the Chinese temple of Leng Noi Yee. The temple is very popular with locals, who make offerings of everything from lotus to gold leaf, incense and rich foods. Returning to Soi 16, continue through an even more exotic food market, which ends in Chinese funerary supplies shops that sell paper objects to be burned with the dead. At the end of the street turn right onto Thanon Phlabphlachi, with shops selling red and gold shrines of all sizes. Turn left on Thanon Charoen Krung (New Road) and follow it as far as the fountain on the square, then turn left onto Thanon Traimit to find Wat Traimit on the left.

If the foodstalls all over Chinatown are too public for you, try the great dim-sum lunches at the Shangarila or at the restaurant at the White Orchid Hotel on Thanon Yaowarat (➤ 68).

INFORMATION

Distance 1½ miles (2½km)
Time 3 hours, excluding stops
Start/end point
★ Tha Ratchawong pier
🚌 D10
🚍 A/C bus 507
🚤 Tha Ratchawong pier
End point Wat Traimit
🚌 E10
🚍 A/C bus 507

Bangkok by Night

Above: *A street vendor displays her colorful barrow at the busy night market*
Above right: *Democracy Monument at night*

WHAT'S ON

Bangkok's English-language daily newspapers have listings of all the cultural events. The monthly *Metro* magazine, available from bookshops, is good for listings as well as notices about new bars, restaurants or shops. Several free listings magazines, including *Where*, *Mustard* and *BK Magazine* can be found in trendy bars and restaurants. The Cultural Information Service (☎ 0 2247 0028) has a schedule of cultural events in English. Tickets can be booked at www.thaiticketmaster.com

BARS AND NIGHTCLUBS

Until a few years ago, Bangkok did not sleep, but now, under strong protest, a 1am closing time has been imposed on bars and nightclubs to clean up its nightlife. The Thai element of *sanuk* (fun, pleasure) that drove the wild nightlife scene before is still there however. Most locals prefer to hang out in the city's many bars, often with live music and usually with food. Arty students and backpackers hang around the lively scene in Banglamphu. Silom Road attracts mainly local workers and foreigners and it has some excellent bar-restaurants. The *sois* (lanes) off Sukhumwit Road are mostly where the more upmarket bars and restaurants are found, except for the rather sleezy Nana Plaza and Soi Cowboy. The more expensive nightclubs, with entrance charges, attract wealthy young Thais and foreigners.

AN EVENING STROLL

Walk through Patpong and Silom Road's night market. Watch out for the cheap fakes, from Rolexes, T-shirts and DVDs to the latest Gameboy games and Vuitton suitcases. After a meal on Soi Ruam Ruedi (▶ 70–71) stroll through the market at Sukhumwit Road Soi 5.

ROMANTIC BANGKOK

For a romantic al fresco meal take a dinner cruise on the Chao Phraya river (▶ 66) and see the floodlit Grand Palace and Wat Arun, or have dinner on the terrace of one of the five-star hotels overlooking the river.

BANGKOK's
top 25 sights

The sights are shown on the maps on the inside front cover and inside back cover, numbered **1**–**25** across the city

Royal Barge Museum

Top and above: Elaborate detail on the royal barges

HIGHLIGHTS

- *Suphannahongsa*, the largest of the royal barges
- The serpent-headed prow of *Anantanagaraj*
- View along Klong Bangkok Noi

INFORMATION

www.thailandmuseum.com
- A7; Locator map A2
- 80/1 Soi Rim Klong Bangkok Noi
- 0 2424 0004
- Daily 9–5
- Restaurants and bar
- A/C bus 3, 7, 9, 11, 124
- Cross the river at Tha Phra Chan pier to Bangkok Noi (Thonburi) train station pier or water-taxi from Tha Chang pier
- Few Inexpensive
- Grand Palace (➤ 31), Wat Phra Kaeo ➤ 32), Sanam Luang (➤ 34)

During December you might see the gilded barges crossing the Chao Phraya to honor King Bhumibol's birthday, but it's not an annual event. Use your imagination to bring them alive as they sit in this boathouse.

Boats for a king Just as royalty now drives around in beautiful cars, so Thai kings used splendidly carved boats as their everyday transportation in the days when Bangkok was very much the "Venice of the East." The grandest of all the royal boats in the museum, the *Suphannahongsa* (golden swan), was first used in 1911 by King Rama VI. It is 148ft (45m) long, intricately carved and gilded, and was reserved exclusively for the king, who sat under the gold canopy in the center. The prow rears up into a mythical swan-like bird known as a *hongsa*. Manned by more than 50 oarsmen, it must have been a wonderful sight as it passed Wat Arun and the riverfront of the Royal Palace. Once in a while—as, for example, at the commemoration of King Bhumibol's 50th anniversary on the throne in December 1996—the *Suphannahongsa* and her sister boats are launched on the river as the centerpiece of grand celebrations.

Boats for lesser mortals The second-largest barge in the shed is the *Anantanagaraj*. It is beautifully carved and has a seven-headed *naga* serpent at its prow. Around it are others from the royal fleet—when 19th-century Thai kings went out, they were accompanied by hundreds of vessels. Among them is a barge similar to the one sent to greet the British diplomat Sir John Bowring, who had been sent to make a trade pact with the king in 1855. The barge had "the gilded and emblazoned image of an idol at its prow, with two flags like vanes grandly ornamented…"

Klong Bangkok Yai

One of the best ways to escape the hell of Bangkok's traffic is to take to the water—a swimming pool, a ride on the riverbus, or a trip on the canals. Klong Bangkok Yai leads from the Chao Phraya to the treasures of Thonburi.

From the river The easiest and cheapest way of getting along Klong Bangkok Yai is on one of the regular long-tail boats from either Tian or Rajini piers on the Chao Phraya. On the right (north) bank as you enter the canal lies Wat Sang Krachai, dating from the Ayutthaya period and restored by early Chakri kings. As you pass under the first of Thonburi's main bridges, look for Wat Welurachin on the left bank, noted for its 19th-century murals. Beyond the next bridge is Wat Inthararam (left bank), containing the ashes of King Taksin, who moved the Siamese capital to Thonburi in 1768 where he was deposed and killed 14 years later. Note the beautiful lacquer decorations on the doors in the ordination hall.

Back to the river At the junction of Klong Sanam Chai and Bangkok Noi sits Wat Pak Nam, a huge temple from the Ayutthaya period, noted for its meditation center. From here Klong Bangkok Yai curves north until it meets Klong Bang Noi (left) and Klong Mon (right), which leads back to the Chao Phraya river. Continuing straight across this junction, Klong Bangkok Yai is called Klong Chak Phra and leads, in a great arc, to Klong Bangkok Noi, and thence to the Royal Barge Museum and the Chao Phraya river.

HIGHLIGHTS

- Life and boats along the *klongs*
- Murals in Wat Welurachin
- Wat Inthararam's painted doors
- Amulets from Wat Pak Nam

INFORMATION

- B9; Locator map A3
- Floating foodstalls along the *klong*
- Regular boats from Tha Phra Chan, Tha Tien and Memorial Bridge piers
- Few
- Royal Barge Museum (▶ 26), Wat Arun (▶ 29), Chao Phraya river (▶ 30)

Top and below: Daily pursuits on the river

Wat Ra Kang

HIGHLIGHTS

- Woodcarvings in the library
- Murals of the *Ramakien*
- Views of the Grand Palace

INFORMATION

- B8; Locator map A2
- Soi Wat Ra Kang Khositaram, off Thanon Arun Amarin
- Daily 7am–9pm
- Express boat to Chang pier, then cross-river ferry to Wat Ra Kang
- None Free
- Royal Barge Museum (► 26), Wat Arun (► 29), Chao Phraya river (► 30)

Exquisite murals

Claims that the Ayutthaya period was one of the high points of Thai art are supported by this undervisited temple, delightfully situated on the banks of the river. Its murals and woodcarvings are exceptionally fine.

Bell temple Most vacationers overlook this delightful smaller *wat*, which dates from the Ayutthaya period, as does its neighbor Wat Arun (► 29). King Taksin undertook serious restorations when he settled in Thonburi, and Rama I rebuilt it extensively. *Rakang* means bell, and at 8am and 6pm every day the *wat's* many bells are rung. The lovely garden feels far removed from bustling Bangkok and is a great place to rest, to enjoy the cross-river view of the Grand Palace, or even to meditate.

A royal present The beautiful library on the compound of Wat Ra Kang was a gift from Rama I to the temple after he founded the Chakri Dynasty. He lived in this elegant 18th-century teak building before he became king, and carried out extensive renovations at the time. The building was suffering from neglect a few years ago, and was restored by the Association of Siamese Architects. The stucco and carved wooden doors and window panels are incredibly fine examples of the Ayutthaya style, depicting figures from the epic *Ramakien*, the Thai interpretation of the Indian Hindu *Ramayana* story. Both the doors and the murals on the interior walls—the work of the great priest-painter Phra Acharn Nak—are considered by art historians to be among the finest in Bangkok.

Wat Arun (Temple of Dawn)

Despite the competition from many skyscrapers fighting for space on Bangkok's skyline, the glittering towers of the Temple of Dawn rise tall above the river. Don't miss the sweeping views from its higher terraces.

The temple of Arun King Taksin chose this 17th-century *wat* for his royal temple and palace as it was the first place in Thonburi to catch the morning light. The Emerald Buddha was housed here after it was recaptured from Laos, before being moved to Wat Phra Kaeo in 1785. Even without the sacred statue, Wat Arun continued to be much revered, and the kings Rama II and Rama III reconstructed and enlarged it to its present height of 341ft (104m). Today, the *wat* has a long, elongated, Khmer-style *prang* (tower), and four minor towers, symbolizing Mount Meru, the terrestrial representation of the 33 heavens. The *prangs* are covered with pieces of porcelain, which Chinese boats coming to Bangkok used as ballast.

The main prang Steep steps lead to the two terraces that form the base of the *prang*, now restored to its full splendor. The different layers, or heavens, are supported by *kinnari*, or half-humans, and frightening *yakshas*, or demons. Pavilions on the first platform contain statues of the Buddha at the most important stages of his life, while on the second terrace four statues of the Hindu god Indra stand guard.

Quiet stroll Most tourists come for the climb and don't have time for the rest of the *wat*, so it is a quiet place for a stroll. The main Buddha image inside the *bot* (chapel) is believed to have been designed by Rama II himself, but the murals date from the reign of Rama V.

HIGHLIGHTS

- Central *prang*
- Close-up of the Chinese porcelain decoration on the *prangs*
- Main Buddha image inside the *bot*

Statue at the temple, a classic image of the city

INFORMATION

www.watarun.com

- B9; Locator map A3
- 34 Thanon Arun Amarin, Bangkok Yai
- 0 2465 5640
- Daily 7.30–5.30
- Foodstalls on the riverbank
- Express boat to Tha Tian pier, then cross-river ferry
- None
- Inexpensive

29

Mae Nam Chao Phraya

The Chao Phraya river, Bangkok's main artery, is a wonderful balm. To board a boat, sniff the breeze and see the grand buildings lining the banks is one of the most exciting, unique and soothing experiences in Bangkok.

The river of kings You can learn much about the history of Bangkok from the Chao Phraya, for it is a city that was designed to be seen from the water: A hundred years ago you would have arrived upriver from the sea port rather than across the city from the airport. Besides the Grand Palace, look out for other buildings connected to the present Chakri Dynasty. These include the Royal Barge Museum, remains of two forts, Chakrabongse House, Wat Ra Kang, Sipakorn University and a couple of royal residences between Krung Thon and Phra Pokklao bridges, one of which was the childhood home of Queen Sirikit.

The river of the people The more congested road traffic becomes, the more people in Bangkok dream of returning to their river. Older inhabitants, in the shadow of the many new glass and concrete highrises, are still living waterborne lives in stilt-houses and on barges, dependent on the brown river for their washing, fishing and transportation. People living on barges near Krung Thep Bridge (past the Marriott Royal Garden Riverside Hotel) trade in charcoal, while others work at the rice warehouses across the river. Further upstream, look for market traders around Pak Klong Talaat and teak loggers with their goods moored around Krung Thon Bridge, waiting for it to be milled and exported. This is some of the best spectator sport Bangkok has to offer and, happily, you are never far from a choice of refreshment.

Grand Palace

The palace, home to the Thai royal family until 1946, is undoubtedly grand, but to appreciate its full splendor is difficult with so many jewels cramped into a relatively small area. Still, the effect is overwhelming.

The oldest building When King Rama I moved from Thonburi to Rattanakosin his plan was to construct an exact copy of the destroyed Ayutthaya. First he built himself a palace and a royal temple, Wat Phra Kaeo (► 32). The oldest buildings are the Maha Montien and the Dusit Maha Prasad, the first brick building (1789) constructed in typical Thai style. Intended as an audience hall, it is now the resting place for deceased royals before the official cremation on Sanam Luang (► 34).

The foreigner The magnificent Chakri Maha Prasad, designed by British architects, is often referred to as "the *farang* (foreigner) with the *chada* (head-dress worn by Thai dancers)," as the main building, in imperial Victorian style, is topped with three Thai spires. The ground level houses a display of weapons, while on the next level there is the Throne Hall and impressive Reception Hall. The top floor contains the ashes of members of the royal family.

Model changes The Wat Phra Kaeo Museum houses tiny Buddha images in precious materials and models showing alterations that have been made to the palace and Wat Phra Kaeo from their beginnings to the modern day. The Amarin Vinichai Prasad (Coronation Hall), built by Rama I and expanded by Rama II and III, is part of the Maha Montien, and is traditionally the room in which each king spends the night after his coronation.

HIGHLIGHTS

- Chakri Maha Prasad
- The garden
- Wat Phra Kaeo Museum
- Amarin Vinichai Prasad (Coronation Hall)
- Dusit Maha Prasad

Decoration fit for a king

INFORMATION

www.palaces.thai.net
- B8/9; Locator map A3
- Thanon Nophralan
- 0 2222 0094
- Daily 8.30–3.30
- Krisa Coffee Shop
- A/C bus 508, 512
- Tha Chang pier Good
- Moderate; includes the Grand Palace, Coin Pavilion, Wat Phra Kaeo and Vimanmek Palace. Personal audioguide in several languages (100B)
- Dress modestly—no shorts, vests or sandals. Shoes and clothes can be rented at the office

31

Wat Phra Kaeo

HIGHLIGHTS

- Murals in the Chapel Royal
- The Emerald Buddha
- Mural of the *Ramakien*

INFORMATION

- B8; Locator map A2
- Thanon Nophralan
- 0 2623 5500
- Daily 8.30–3.30
- A/C bus 508, 512
- Tha Chang pier
- None
- Included in entrance to Grand Palace. Dress modestly and cover arms and legs

Splendid uniformed demons stand guard

Wat Phra Kaeo, Temple of the Emerald Buddha, reveals some of the most stunning architecture in all Southeast Asia. It also explains the tradition of firm belief the Thai people have in the Buddhist religion and in their nation.

The Emerald Buddha Wat Phra Kaeo is the holiest of all Thai *wats*, and the small green-jade statue of the Buddha, high on its golden altar in the Chapel Royal, is the most sacred image in Thailand. When the statue was first found in 1434 it was covered in stucco. Years later, the stucco started to crumble away and several miracles occurred, giving the Buddha a reputation for bringing good fortune. Today, thousands of worshippers pay their respects in front of the statue. The late Ayutthaya-style murals on the surrounding walls depict the lives of Buddha, and the superb door panels with mother-of-pearl inlay illustrate scenes from the *Ramakien*, the Thai version of the Indian *Ramayana*. The golden outer walls and gilded angels reflect the sun, while bells along the roofline give voice to the wind.

More temples and murals On the upper terrace next to the Chapel Royal are three other very sacred buildings: the Royal Pantheon, surrounded by gilded *kinaree* (male) and *kinara* (female) half-human figures; the Library, which holds the *Tripitaka*, the sacred Buddhist scriptures; and the impressive golden Phra Si Ratana *chedi* (pagoda), which houses ashes of Buddha. The nearby model of Angkor Wat is a reminder that Cambodia was once under Thai rule. The whole ground is enclosed by galleries decorated with murals depicting the *Ramakien*.

Pipitaphan (National Museum)

You'll need at least three hours, but preferably a whole day, to come to terms with this astonishing collection of Thai art and archeology. Most of the museum's buildings, too, are works of art in their own right.

Oldest letters The museum, founded in 1874 by King Rama V, is housed in the Palace of Prince Wang Na, originally home to the Second King and part of the Grand Palace (► 31). The visit starts with a useful introduction to Thai history. Note the black-stone inscription from Sukhothai, the oldest-known record of the Thai alphabet. Two large modern buildings house the main collection of pre-Thai and Thai sculpture, as well as pieces from elsewhere in Asia. An important exhibit in the southern wing is one of the earliest images of Buddha, from Gandhara in India, and is clearly influenced by classical Greek sculpture. A garage in a nearby building houses the collection of magnificent royal funeral chariots, the most amazing being the *Vejayant Rajarot*, built by Rama I in 1785 and still occasionally used, even though it needs 300 men to pull it.

Palace of Wang Na Built in the 1780s as a home for the king's successor, the palace houses a magnificent collection of Thai art objects. Note in Room 23 a wonderful collection of traditional musical instruments from Southeast Asia.

Buddhaisawan Chapel The Phra Sihing Buddha in this chapel is said to have been divinely created in Sri Lanka and sent to Sukhothai in the 13th century. Despite doubts about its origins (it actually dates from the 15th century), it is still worshiped by many and is carried in procession at the Thai New Year. The fine murals around it tell the stories of Buddha's lives.

HIGHLIGHTS

- Sukhothai sculpture
- *Vejayant Rajarot* chariot
- Red House
- Phra Sihing Buddha
- Murals in the Buddhaisawan Chapel
- Musical instruments and audio tapes in the Palace of Wang Na
- Bronze Bodhisattva Avalokitesvara from Chaya (room 9)

INFORMATION

- ✚ B7/8; Locator map A2
- ✉ Thanon Naphratad 1
- ☎ 0 2224 1370
- 🕐 Wed–Sun 9–4, but check in advance as schedule changes
- 🍴 Café with inexpensive food
- 🚌 A/C bus 503, 506, 507
- 🚢 Tha Pra Chang pier
- ♿ Few
- 💷 Inexpensive
- ❓ Free English tours start at ticket pavilion on Wed at 9.30am (Buddhism) and Thu 9.30am (Thai art and culture); on other days tours are in German, French and Japanese. For information ☎ 0 2224 1370

Sanam Luang (Royal Field)

Just north of the Grand Palace are the royal cremation grounds, today most often used for picnics. Lak Muang, foodstalls and many shady trees here offer a nice place to relax after an exhausting visit to the adjoining sights.

Royal cremation grounds This vast green field near the Grand Palace was originally designed as the funeral grounds for royal members of the Chakri Dynasty. The last ceremonial cremations, attended by more than 4,000 people, took place in March 1996 for the funeral of the mother of the present King Bhumibol. Sanam Luang is also the site of the annual Plowing Ceremony (► 4), when the king marks the beginning of the rice-growing season, and for the celebrations of King Bhumibol's birthday on 5 December (► 4). The statue of the earth goddess, Mae Thorani, in a pavilion on the northern side, was erected by King Chulalongkorn as part of a public fountain.

Lak Muang (City Pillar Shrine) This lovely shrine, believed to be inhabited by the spirit that protects Bangkok, is built around two Sivaite *lingam* wooden pillars erected by Rama I in 1782 to mark the founding of his new capital. Thais believe their wishes will be granted if they worship at the shrine. It is known for its powers to grant fertility to those who come here to make offerings of pig heads and incense. Thai dancers are commissioned to perform here and to thank the deities for granting a wish.

Kite fights The green space is now mainly used for recreation. People come here for family picnics, to rest, to play ball games and to fly kites. There are regular kite competitions between February and May.

Wat Po

After a visit to the Grand Palace or a day's shopping in Chinatown or Sukhumwit, there's nothing as relaxing as a visit to the beautiful temple compound of Wat Po and a vigorous Thai massage to get you back on your feet.

The Reclining Buddha Wat Po was built in the 16th century during the Ayutthaya period and almost completely rebuilt in 1781 by Rama I. It is Bangkok's oldest and Thailand's largest *wat*. Thanon Chethuphon divides the grounds in two, one side comprising the temple buildings and the other the monks' quarters. The temple's main attraction is the giant Reclining Buddha, 151-ft (46m) long and 49-ft (15m) high, which represents the dying Buddha in the position he adopted to attain nirvana. The statue was built in the 19th century during the reign of Rama III, from brick covered with lacquer, plaster and gold leaf. The soles of the feet are decorated in mother-of-pearl with 108 signs of Buddha. The beautiful *bot*, or central shrine, has delicately carved sandstone panels representing the *Ramakien* and the finest mother-of-pearl inlaid doors. Although Wat Po contains 91 *chedis*, the four most important are dedicated to the first Chakri kings. Visitors can acquire merit by putting a coin in each of the 108 bronze bowls.

Center of learning Rama III wanted this temple to be used for education, and Thais still consider it their first public university. The murals in the *viharn* and other buildings explain a wide variety of subjects, such as geography, yoga, astrology, science, literature and arts, as well as religion. Today, the temple complex still includes the Traditional Medical Practitioners' Association (▶ 59), which teaches the traditional art of Thai massage and herbal remedies.

The Reclining Buddha (top) and gilded detail (above) at Wat Po

DID YOU KNOW?

- 95 percent of Thais practise Theravada Buddhism, also known as "the lesser vehicle"
- The ultimate destination of Theravada Buddhism is nirvana
- Most Thais pray, donate and gain merit at temples in the hope of acquiring rebirth in a better life

INFORMATION

- ✚ B/C9; Locator map A3
- ✉ Thanon Maha Rat
- ☎ 0 2221 1375
- ⏱ Daily 8–6, massage until 5
- 🚌 A/C bus 506, 507, 508, 512
- ⛴ Tha Tian pier
- ♿ Good
- 💰 Inexpensive

35

Talaad Pak Klong

Thailand's biggest flower market is one of Bangkok's most colorful places. The atmosphere is frenetic in the early morning and during festival seasons—proof that flowers are still important in Thai culture.

Busy market Garland makers and florists come to the market in early morning for the freshest buds delivered from gardens and plantations outside the city. Thanon Jakapetch runs straight through the market, with cars and *tuk-tuks* on both sides filled with flowers. Wholesalers and retailers meet here over myriad smells and colors—of flowers, vegetables and fruit. The fruit market is separate from the flower market, which is divided into areas dedicated to particular flowers: roses, marigolds, lilies, *dok ruk* (a Thai white flower much used in garlands), perfumed jasmine and, of course, more orchids than you have ever seen. At night the market is slightly calmer but lovely with all the stalls lit up.

Malai **(flower garland)** *Malais* are sold very cheaply here, near temples, other markets or at traffic intersections. These garlands, strung with jasmine buds, rose petals, orchids, crown flower (*dok rul*) or marigolds, are very important in Thai society, both for the worldly pleasure they offer and as an expression of religious piety. Thais who buy a garland, cup their hands together in a *wai* upon receiving it. They offer the garland, together with lotus flowers, to honor the virtue of Lord Buddha. Garlands are also used as a decoration for weddings and funerals, a hair ornament, an air-freshener, or as a token of respect. The majority of *malais* are made by street vendors but the most exquisite ones are made by the palace ladies, who make them as their ancestors did 700 years ago in Sukhotai.

DID YOU KNOW?

- It can take a skilled floral artist and two assistants more than 12 hours to make a complicated *malai*
- Garlands are symbols of love and devotion because they take so long to prepare
- Queen Sirikit Park in Chatuchak (► 62) is a botanical garden where many native flowers and plants are grown, including the Wringntia Sirikitiae Mid flower, unique to Thailand

INFORMATION

- ✛ C9; Locator map A3
- ✉ Thanon Chakraphet, near Memorial Bridge
- 🕙 Daily 24 hours
- 🍴 Foodstalls
- 🚌 A/C bus 506
- 🚤 Tha Saphan Phut
- ✋ Free
- ↔ Chao Phraya river (► 30), Wat Po (► 35), Grand Palace (► 31), Wat Phra Kaeo (► 32)

Wat Prayoon

There is something surreal about this temple complex in the shadow of the old Memorial Bridge, with its giant *chedi*, artificial hill of miniature shrines and turtles partial to the taste of tourist fingers (be warned).

Distinctive pagodas Wat Prayoon, known locally under its longer name of Wat Prayun Rawongsawat, was built during the reign of Rama III by the powerful local Bunnag family. Its huge gray *chedis* (pagodas) are easily recognized from the river and Memorial Bridge. The *wat* has some fine mother-of-pearl inlaid doors.

Turtle Mount To the right as you enter is an artifical hill, circled clockwise by worshipers. It was constructed by King Rama III after he observed the shapes made by candle wax as it melted. Between the strange shapes are shrines to the dead in different styles, from the most traditional Thai-style *chedi* to a cowboy ranch complete with cacti. The thousands of turtles in the pond surrounding the shrines gave the mount its name. Vendors sell bread and fruit for these greedy creatures—locals believe special merit is gained by feeding them. Sticks are available to ensure that the turtles don't eat your fingers too. At the edge of the pond is a memorial to the unfortunate men who died in 1836 when one of the temple's cannons exploded.

Twins Bangkok's first European-style house, home of British trader Robert Hunter, used to stand in front of the *wat*. In 1824 Hunter saw the original "Siamese" (conjoined) twins, Chang and Eng, swimming in the river nearby. The twins left Siam in 1829, and married two American sisters with whom they had 22 children. They died in 1874 within two hours of each other.

DID YOU KNOW?

* Just upstream of Memorial Bridge is the Catholic Church of Santa Cruz, the core of the old Portuguese quarter
* Several Portuguese churches still exist today, including the Church of the Immaculate Conception (1837) near Krung Thon Bridge and the Holy Rosary Church (1787)

INFORMATION

* ✚ C10; Locator map A3
* ✉ Soi 1, off Thanon Thetsaban, Thonburi
* 🕐 Daily 9–6
* 🚢 Tha Saphan Phot pier, then walk over Memorial Bridge
* ♿ None
* ✋ Free; inexpensive turtle food

Wat Saket

It's easy to get lost in the grounds of this vast, peaceful temple, but the short, steep climb up the Golden Mount puts everything in perspective and offers unparalleled views over Rattanakosin—the Royal City (► 22).

The chedi, built on the Golden Mount in 1863

HIGHLIGHTS

- Views over Rattanakosin
- Murals in the main chapel
- Temple fair in November
- Tiny bird and antique market

INFORMATION

- ✚ D8; Locator map B2
- ✉ Off Thanon Bamrung Muang
- ☎ 0 2223 4561
- 🕐 Daily 8–5
- 🚌 A/C bus 511, 512
- ⛴ Water-taxis on Klong San Sap and Klong Maha Nak
- ♿ None
- 💲 Free; inexpensive donation for top of Golden Mount

Golden Mount The main attraction of this temple is the Golden Mount (Phu Khao Thong). The artificial hill, nearly 262-ft (80-m) high, was created in the early 19th century after a large *chedi* built by Rama III collapsed when the underlying ground gave way. Only a huge pile of rubble was left, but as Buddhists believe that a religious building should never be destroyed, King Rama IV had 1,000 teak logs put into the foundations. Later, he built a small *chedi* on top of the hill, which is believed to contain Buddha's teeth. During World War II, concrete walls were added to prevent any further erosion. Views from the terrace on top of the hill are wonderful, and you are allowed into the golden *chedi*. Every year (first week of November) a fabulous temple fair takes place, when believers hold a solemn candle-lit procession up the illuminated Golden Mount.

Temple complex The temple was built outside the city walls by King Rama I during the late 18th century as the city's main crematory. The king performed the Royal Hair Bathing Ceremony here before he was crowned. When plague raged through the city in the 19th century, the temple became a charnel house and more than 60,000 victims were left here to the vultures. The temple building itself is not very interesting, but the fine murals inside the main temple are worth a close inspection. There are two important old Buddha statues in the Shrine Hall.

Chinatown

Chinatown's busy, intricate alleyways may no longer be lined with brothels and opium dens, but its amazing markets and temples, the latter shrouded in incense clouds, still give the feel of a world apart, even in Bangkok.

The Chinese community By the 14th century Chinese merchants had set up important trading centers in Thailand and were the only foreigners allowed to live within the walls of Ayutthaya. The Chinese were already well established in Bangkok when King Rama I built his capital on their grounds in 1782 and moved them to the Sampeng area. For a long time Chinatown was the city's commercial center, also gaining notoriety for its brothels, teahouses and opium dens. The restored Chalermkrung Royal Theater on Thanon Charoen Krung is a perfect example of the theaters in the area. Chinese temples seem more down to earth than their Thai counterparts, one of the liveliest being Leng Noi Yee (➤ 23), which means "Dragon Lotus Temple." It has Buddhist, Taoist and Confucianist altars, and you will find old Chinese men playing chess and watching the crocodiles in Wat Chakrawat.

Street markets Chinatown reveals its true soul in its street markets, old shophouses and shopping streets. The busiest alleyways are Soi Wanit 1 (Sampeng Lane) and Soi Isaraphap (➤ 23), and through the heart of it all cuts Thanon Yaowarat, famous for its gold shops. Nakorn Kasem, the so-called Thieves' Market (➤ 55), may no longer offer bargains but it is still great for a stroll.

HIGHLIGHTS

- Soi Wanit 1 (Sampeng Lane)
- Thanon Yaowarat, or "Gold Street"
- Chalermkrung Royal Theater
- Wat Chakrawat
- Nakorn Kasem (Thieves' Market)
- Soi Isaraphap
- Leng Noi Yee Temple

INFORMATION

- ✚ D9/10; Locator map B3
- 🍴 Street stalls, food markets, White Orchid Hotel for excellent dim sum (➤ 68)
- 🚌 A/C bus 507
- ⛴ Tha Ratchawong pier
- ♿ Few
- ↔ Wat Traimit (➤ 42)

Phra Thi Nang Wimanmek

HIGHLIGHTS

- Guided tour through the house
- Garden and pond
- Trophy Room
- Ivory objects in the library

INFORMATION

- ✚ E6; Locator map C1
- ✉ 193/2 Thanon Ratchawithi
- ☎ 0 2628 6300
- ⏰ Daily 9.30–4 (tickets sold until 3.30). Visitors wearing shorts or sleeveless shirts may not be admitted as this is a royal property. Abhisek Dusit Throne Hall: daily 1–4
- 🍴 Cafeteria in grounds and Thai restaurant near crafts shop
- 🚌 A/C bus 503, 510
- ⛴ Tha Thuwet pier
- ♿ Few
- 💲 Moderate; free with entrance ticket for Grand Palace and Wat Phra Keo (➤ 31, 32)
- ❓ Compulsory, free hour-long guided tours of the palace in English and other languages every half-hour. Performances of Thai dancing, Thai boxing and sword- and club-fighting at 10.30am and 2pm

A tour through Vimanmek Palace, the world's largest golden teak mansion, gives an insight into the interests of the Thai royal family. The beautiful landscaped gardens are a great place for whiling away the afternoon heat.

"The Palace in the Clouds" The three-story mansion was originally built in 1868 as a summer house on the island of Ko Si Chang. It was moved to Dusit in 1901 and, quite understandably, soon became King Rama V's favorite palace and was used as the royal residence between 1902 and 1906. It was closed down in 1935 and remained in this state until Queen Sirikit re-opened it in 1982 as a museum to mark Bangkok's bicentennial celebrations.

First bathroom Although European influence is clearly visible in the style, Vimanmek is built according to Thai traditions, using golden teak wood and not a single nail. Teak wood contains a special oil that makes it resistant to heat and heavy rains, and which also acts as an insect repellent. Amongst the possessions of Rama V on display is Thailand's first indoor bathroom and the oldest typewriter with Thai characters, as well as Thai ceramics, European furniture, precious china and lovely portraits.

Carriages and crafts The Royal Carriage Museum contains carriages, mostly imported from Europe, which were popular at the time of Rama V. The small Suan Farang Kunsai Mansion has oil paintings and pictures of Rama V and his family. The Abhisek Dusit Throne Hall, built in a harmonious Euro-Thai style, has a display of handicrafts, such as *mutmee* silk, nielloware and basketry, made by Queen Sirikit's SUPPORT Foundation.

Oriental Hotel

There are hotels, and then there's the Oriental. Arrive by car, acknowledge the greetings of the hotel's efficient white-uniformed staff, pass through the great glass doors into the lobby, and you'll be touched by its magic.

Romantic past Nothing remains of the original 1876 Oriental, but the Authors' Residence, dwarfed by two more modern wings, is the surviving building of 1887. This section contains the hotel's most luxurious suites, named after such illustrious guests as Somerset Maugham, Graham Greene and Noel Coward, and continues to attract modern celebrities such as David Bowie and Tom Cruise. The street-level lounge of this colonial building, surrounded by exclusive boutiques, is a great place to escape to on a hot afternoon to take traditional English afternoon tea.

Luxurious present Elsewhere in the hotel, excellence vies with elegance. If you want to have a look around, go at sunset for a drink on the terrace or an al fresco dinner at the excellent riverside buffet. Alternatively, catch the hotel's ferry across the busy river to the splendid Sala Rim Naam for good Thai food (▶ 66) and a performance of classical Thai music and dance. If you want to get more involved, there is a world-class cookery school where you can see how your favorite Thai dishes are prepared, and an excellent cultural program run by university professors. The luxurious spa, set in a traditional teak house, offers every imaginable treat to soothe or stimulate the body (▶ 58–59).

DID YOU KNOW?

- The Royal Suite occupies the entire top floor
- The Oriental is consistently voted one of the world's best hotels

INFORMATION

www.mandarinoriental.com
- 🔲 E11; Locator map C4
- ✉ 48 Soi Oriental
- ☎ 0 2659 9000
- 🍴 Restaurants and bar
- 🚇 Skytrain: Saphan Taksin (free shuttle boat to the hotel)
- 🚢 Tha Oriental pier
- ♿ Good
- ↔ Wat Arun (▶ 29), Chao Phraya river (▶ 30)
- ❓ Smart casual dress. Hotel residency not necessary for spa and classes

Top and below: Refined luxury at the Oriental

Wat Traimit

DID YOU KNOW?

- Every Buddha image should be treated with respect
- Some of Thailand's finest art was produced during the Sukhothai period (13th–15th centuries)
- Sukhothai Buddhas are usually seated with hands in the Bhumisparsa Mudra position, the right hand touching the earth and the left resting in the lap

INFORMATION

- ✚ E10; Locator map C3
- ✉ Thanon Traimit, off Thanon Charoen Krung, Chinatown
- ☎ 0 2623 1226
- 🕐 Daily 9–5
- 🍴 Foodstalls in Chinatown
- 🚌 Bus 25, 53, 40
- 🚢 Tha Ratchawong pier
- ♿ None 💲 Inexpensive
- ↔ Chinatown (► 39)

Top: The Golden Buddha Right: A less valuable gold-leaf version

You know when you have arrived at Wat Traimit, the Temple of the Golden Buddha, as the entrance is always blocked with tour buses. But no matter how many tourists invade, the Golden Buddha remains unruffled.

The Golden Buddha The shiny, 10-ft (3-m) tall gold Buddha, which weighs 7.4 tons, is believed to be the largest golden Buddha image in the world. The sculpture, made in Sukhothai in the 13th century, was covered with stucco to protect it from the Burmese invaders of the 18th century. It wasn't until 1955, when workmen moved the Buddha image to a new building and saw through some cracks that there was something shining beneath the surface, that the stucco was taken off and solid gold revealed. The discovery sparked a national treasure hunt, but nothing of similar value was found. Historically, the Golden Buddha has nothing to do with the Chinese community, but it seems more than appropriate that it has found its home in Chinatown, which is, after all, the center of Bangkok's gold trade. The statue is now valued at US $14 million, and several bits of stucco are on display to the left of it.

A less impressive temple The temple itself probably dates from the early 13th century. The statue of Reverend Phra Visutha-Thibordee, the abbot who ordered the construction of the new temple for the Golden Buddha, sits just opposite it and is covered in gold leaf.

Baan Jim Thompson

Although it is a great introduction to traditional Thai architecture, Jim Thompson's House clearly shows Western influences. The landscaped garden and views offer a welcome surprise after bustling Siam Square.

One of the many Asian works of art Thompson acquired on his travels

The lost adventurer American architect Jim Thompson first came to Thailand during World War II. As he couldn't get used to his uneventful life back in New York after the war, he decided to make Thailand his home. Thai culture and crafts fascinated him, but the day he discovered some silk-weavers near his house (► 74, panel) his fortune was secured. He was already something of a legend when, in 1967, he disappeared mysteriously during an afternoon walk in the Cameron Highlands in Malaysia, never to be seen again. Thompson's friend, the prolific author William Warren, wrote a great account of his life and death, *Jim Thompson: The Legendary American of Thailand* (Jim Thompson Thai Silk Company, Bangkok, 1970).

Thai-style residence Thompson bought six traditional teak houses in northern and central Thailand, and had them reassembled in Bangkok as his residence, adding Western elements such as stairways and marble floors. The exterior walls were turned inside out to face the interior, and the garden was lovingly landscaped, creating the effect of a peaceful but abundant oasis.

A wonderful collection The spirit of the house, kept as Thompson left it, makes an ideal background for his small but gorgeous display of Asian art. The collection of traditional Thai paintings is one of the best in the world and there are also some very rare Buddha images.

HIGHLIGHTS

- Teak Ayutthaya architecture
- Exotic landscaped garden
- Views over the *klong*
- Asian art collection
- Traditional Thai paintings

INFORMATION

www.jimthompson.com

⊞ F8; Locator map D3

✉ Soi Kasem San 2, off Thanon Rama I, Siam Square

☎ 0 2216 7368

🕐 Daily 9–5

🚉 Skytrain: National Stadium

🚤 Water-taxi from Wat Saket (► 38) along Klong San Sap to Thanon Phrauathai

♿ None

💷 Moderate (guided tours only)

43

Thanon Patpong

INFORMATION

➕ G11; Locator map D4

✉ Soi Patpong 1, 2, 3, 4, between Thanon Silom and Thanon Surawong

🕐 Most exciting after sunset until 1am

🍴 Many good restaurants (▶ 64–71) and countless foodstalls

🚇 Skytrain: Sala Daeng

🚌 A/C bus 502, 504

♿ None

Patpong—two parallel streets and a lane running between Thanon Silom and Thanon Surawong—is renowned as a vibrant nightlife center, but also offers a busy night market, good bookstores and several restaurants.

The strip that never used to sleep Patpong is most busy in the evening. By day it's another Bangkok shopping street of bookstores, pharmacies and supermarkets. Late in the afternoon, foodstalls set up at either end of Patpong, some of them good enough to be reviewed in the city's English-language papers. Then bootleg DVDs and CDs, cotton clothing, fake designer watches and souvenirs are laid out on Soi Patpong 1. Later the street fills with revelers and the restaurants and bars open up until 1am.

Bars and restaurants Patpong is renowned for its go-go bars, discos and late night "constellations." Despite its somewhat unsavory reputation, it's remarkably safe to visit—though it's as well to stick to the downstairs bars, as some of the upper floor establishments have been known to overcharge. Patpong 1 has a few go-go bars but is mainly a shopping street where foreign couples shop and drink. Patpong 2 has numerous smaller beer bars (*ba bia* in Thai), as well as a row of karaoke establishments and the most popular restaurants on the strip. Patpong 3, an unassuming dead-end lane, is more of a gay venue. The strip comes alive in the early evening, but with the exception of a handful of constellations is more-or-less closed down by 1am. Although sex is for sale in Patpong, the area is much more than just a red light area, being frequented by young Thais and foreign visitors who dance, talk and dine into the small hours.

Wang Suan Pakkad

Suan Pakkad Palace is a lovely corner amid urban sprawl, and delights the few visitors who come its way. Like Jim Thompson (➤ 43), its owners were passionate collectors of Thai arts and traditional architecture.

"**Cabbage Farm Palace**" Prince and Princess Chumbhot of Nakhon Sawan moved these seven traditional Thai houses from Chiang Mai (some of them had belonged to the prince's great-grandfather) in 1952. The cabbage garden was turned into one of Bangkok's finest land-scaped gardens and is calm in a uniquely Eastern way. The princess was one of the country's most dedicated art collectors, and the house has been turned into a museum displaying everyday objects such as perfume bottles, betel-nut boxes and musical instruments. Antiques include an exquisite Buddha head from Ayutthaya, Khmer statues and European prints of old Siam.

Ban Chiang House An entire house has been devoted to the elegant pottery and bronze jewelry discovered at Ban Chiang, an important Bronze Age settlement in northern Thailand, dating from around 1600–500BC.

Lacquer Pavilion The exquisite Lacquer Pavilion, once part of an Ayutthaya monastery, was moved here in 1958. The remarkable gold and black lacquer murals depict events from the life of the Buddha and the *Ramakien*, the Thai version of the *Ramayana* epic. The lower layer is notable for its representations of daily life, including the odd *farang* on horseback.

Marsi Gallery This new gallery hosts some of Bangkok's best occasional exhibitions of contemporary art.

HIGHLIGHTS

- Lacquer Pavilion
- Buddha head from Ayutthaya
- Lovely enclosed garden
- Wonderful prints of old Siam by European artists

INFORMATION

- ✚ G8; Locator map E2
- ✉ 352 Thanon Sri Ayudhaya
- ☎ 0 2245 4934
- 🕐 Daily 9–4; Marsi Gallery: daily 9–6 (☎ 0 2245 0568/6368)
- 🍴 Restaurants around Victory Monument
- 🚉 Skytrain: Phaya Thai
- 🚌 A/C bus 14, 17, 38
- ♿ None 🅼 Moderate

The collection of fine art extends into the grounds

Saan Phra Phrom (Erawan Shrine)

DID YOU KNOW?

- Thai Buddhism incorporates elements of Brahmanism, animism and ancestor worship
- A spirit house's location is determined by a Brahmin priest

INFORMATION

- ✚ H9; Locator map E3
- ✉ Corner of Thanon Ratchadamri and Thanon Ploenchit
- 🕐 Early morning–late night
- 🍴 Restaurants nearby
- 🚇 Skytrain: Chit Lom or Ratchadamri
- 🚌 A/C bus 501. 508, 511, 513
- ♿ Good   🎫 Free

The shrine is always strewn with offerings

Surrounded by the trendiest stores, Erawan Shrine is something of a surprise. Yet the old ways of praying and making offerings blend in with the money culture. Classical Thai dancing is performed here for donations.

Spirit house The Erawan Shrine was erected as a spirit house (▶ 34, panel) connected to the Erawan Hotel, which has now made way for the Grand Hyatt Erawan Hotel. The forces of the typical Thai spirit house didn't seem effective enough during the building of the hotel, so spirit doctors advised that it be replaced with the four-headed image of Brahma (Phra Phrom in Thai). There have been no further hitches since then, and the shrine has became famous for bringing good fortune. The name Erawan comes from Brahma's three-headed elephant.

Merit-making People offer colorful flower garlands, lotus flowers, incense and candles; after a few minutes at the shrine your senses tend to go into overdrive. Often, if a wish has been granted, people thank the spirits by donating teak elephants or commissioning the classical dancers and live orchestra. Outside the shrine women sell birds in tiny cages, which are believed to bring good fortune and earn merit if you set them free. Lottery tickets sold by physically impaired vendors at the shrine are thought to be lucky. The variety of worshipers is also surprising: older people more set in their ways, middle-class Thai families with children, and fashionable younger women in the latest Western designer clothes all kneel down to perform the same traditional rites.

Suan Lumphini (Lumphini Park)

At first the park looks rather sad and dusty, but spend time in this demanding city and the value of Lumphini is apparent. It is one of the green places that keep people sane, and allows an insight into how Thais relax.

The park is a peaceful oasis in the hectic city

First light Lumphini is a place of moods rather than sights. In the early morning, before 7am, the park is full of people exercising. More graceful than the joggers are Chinese-led *t'ai chi* groups, making slow movements to music. At this hour traders also sell snake blood, a powerful tonic. Suddenly, all this activity comes to an abrupt halt and everyone stands to attention as the PA system plays the national anthem. By 9am, when the sun is up and rush-hour traffic is souring the air, the crowd thins out.

Last light There's a different crowd in the afternoon. Joggers run on the 1.5 mile (2.5km) track, people pump weights at the open-air gym, and, in the windy season (February to April), kites soar above the busy city—at the height of the season you can buy beautiful kites here. When the light softens so does the atmosphere. Couples come out, foodstalls are set up and boats are rowed on the artificial lake until, at 6pm, with traffic at a halt in the evening rush, people in the park also stand still as the national anthem is played again. The park is especially atmospheric at dusk, when the skyscrapers are silhouetted against the fading light.

DID YOU KNOW?

● Lumphini is Bangkok's biggest inner city park. Other green spaces in the city include: Chatuchak Park, near the weekend market (➤ 48); pleasant Benjasiri Park between Soi 22–25 on Thanon Sukhumwit (➤ 49) and the small Santichaiprakan Park on Thanon Phra Sumen in Banglamphu are popular with locals

INFORMATION

✚ Main entrance: H10/11; Locator map E4
✉ Corner of Thanon Rama IV and Thanon Ratchadamri
🕐 Daily 5am–8pm
🍴 Restaurant and foodstalls on the north side
🚉 Skytrain: Sala Daeng, Ratchadamri
🚌 A/C bus 502, 504, 505
♿ Very good
💲 Free
🔗 Shopping at World Trade Center and Peninsula Plaza (➤ 76, panel), Erawan Shrine (➤ 76), Thanon Sukhumwit (➤ 49)
❓ The boating concession is open 6am–8pm. Avoid dogs at all costs; several people in Lumphini Park have been bitten by rabid dogs

Chatuchak Weekend Market

HIGHLIGHTS

- Amulets and collectors' items, section 1
- Old photos, section 2
- Hill-tribe textiles and crafts, sections 22–6
- Aw Taw Kaw Market, royal project for organically grown produce on other side of Thanon Phahonyothin

Local crafts galore can be found at this huge market

INFORMATION

- ✚ J3; Locator map E1
- ✉ Thanon Phahonyothin, near Chatuchak Park
- 🕐 Sat–Sun 8–6
- 🍴 Foodstalls, D'Jit Pochana, Chamlong Vegetarian Restaurant near bus terminal
- 🚇 Skytrain: Mo Chit
- 🚌 A/C bus 502, 503, 510, 512, 513
- ♿ None 🎟 Free
- ℹ TAT office ✉ Off Thanon Kampong Phet 2

This weekend market feels like the mother of all markets, and if you know where to look you can find everything from baby crocodiles and children's clothes to *mutmee* silk pajamas and antiques.

General view It used to take an hour (or even longer) to get to the market from the center, but it is now much faster with the new expressway and, especially, with the Skytrain. Before going, get hold of Nancy Chandler's *Map of Bangkok* (available from English-language bookstores), which has a detailed map of Chatuchak showing what is for sale where. Many stalls are aimed at tourists, but most cater to Thais who come here looking for food, plants, furnishings, or clothes, or simply for a drink.

Everything for sale If time is limited, start with Sois 1, 2, 3, and 4, which sell antiques, woodcarvings, musical instruments, hill-tribe items, and crafts. The selection of sarongs in cotton and *mutmee* silk is amazing, while clothes by Thai designers are very wearable. The sections around the clocktower have mainly food supplies and, on the other side, household items and live animals.

Illegal trade Regardless of a Thai law protecting endangered species, some endangered animals are still on sale in Chatuchak, branded "the wildlife supermarket of the world" by the Worldwide Fund for Nature. Very few endangered animals are still openly for sale in the market and, if they are, their cages will have signs insisting on "No Photograph." However, the black market is still thriving, and apparently animals such as crocodiles, gibbons, tigers and lion cubs are still for sale as pets, or to be eaten for their supposed medicinal properties.

Thanon Sukhumwit

Sukhumwit Road runs like a long artery through the heart of modern Bangkok, but in the rush hour you can easily get stuck in traffic for an hour or more. In which case the only solution might be to get out and shop.

The wealthy *farang* area At its start near the National Stadium it is called Thanon Rama I, beyond Siam Square it becomes Thanon Ploenchit, and past the bridge of the expressway it finally becomes Thanon Sukhumwit. Several smart shopping malls line Thanon Ploenchit and quite a few of the older embassies lie just off it. Where once *farangs* (foreigners) preferred to live near the river, most now live on the *sois* off Thanon Sukhumwit in pretty villas with gardens or in luxurious apartment blocks.

Shopping Many large shopping centers are on this road. The choicest and most exclusive is the Gaysorn Plaza (▶ 76) on Ploenchit Road, and the elegant Emporium (▶ 76) on Sukhumwit is by far the most popular place to be seen. For a rest from shopping, check out Benjasiri Park, next to the Emporium, where many open-air events are staged. The area around Siam Square is popular with teenagers and this is the place for new Thai designers, young fashion and accessories and fast-food noodle shops. The small streets around Thanon Sukhumwit Soi 23 have some of the more interesting crafts. and away from the traffic they make for a pleasant stroll.

Entertainment Much of the city's nightlife now happens in the *sois* off Sukhumwit Road. Some of the trendiest bar-clubs are on Soi 11, including Zanzibar (▶ 71) and Bed Supper Club (▶ 82). For a different atmosphere head for Little Arabia around Sois 3 and 5.

DID YOU KNOW?

- *Thanon* means "road" or "street," *soi* means "small street" and *drok* means "little alley"
- Some *soi* are also known under their proper names—so, Sukhumwit Soi 21 is Soi Asoke

INFORMATION

- J9–K10 and off map; Locator map F3
- Numerous good restaurants
- Skytrain: Central
- A/C bus 501, 508, 511, 513
- Few
- Space Contemporary Art Gallery ✉ Tai Ping Tower, 582–9 Soi Sukhumwit 63 ☎ 711 4427 ◷ Wed–Sun noon–10pm

Sukhumwit traffic

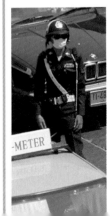

Baan Kam Thieng

▌ **Kam Thieng House, a 19th-century teak stilt-house from Chiang Mai, is increasingly encroached upon by the city. However, its collection gives an interesting glimpse of the rural lifestyle of northern Thailand.**

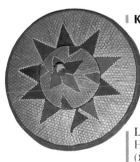

Traditional headwear on show in the museum

HIGHLIGHTS

● Siam Society Library
● Floral lintels above the door to the inner room to ward off evil spirits
● An encounter with the spirits of the three elderly women

INFORMATION

www.siam-society.org
✚ K9/10; Locator map F3
✉ 131 Soi Sukhumwit 21 (Soi Asoke)
☎ 0 2661 6470
🕐 Tue–Sat 9–5. Guided tours in English Sat 9.30am
🍴 Drinks in cafeteria
🚉 Skytrain: Asoke
Ⓜ Sukhumrit
🚌 A/C bus 501, 508, 511, 513
♿ None 🎫 Moderate
❓ The Siam Society has a library, gallery and small office selling its books. For lectures, check the website

Lanna Living Museum Unlike Jim Thompson's House (► 43) and the Suan Pakkad Palace (► 45), Baan Kam Thieng shows how ordinary people lived. It represents a complete northern Thai house with living quarters, kitchen, well, granary, rice pounder, spirit house and household objects and utensils used in the daily life of the people of the north. Farming tools and fish traps are displayed on the street level, while upstairs rooms give a feel of the rural lifestyle of 150 years ago. The house was built by the granddaughter of a wealthy northern prince, and it is believed that her spirit and the spirit of her mother and granddaughter still inhabit the house: There are many stories of inexplicable incidents occurring here.

Saengaroon House The more recently acquired Saengaroon House, originally from Ayutthaya, contains the craft collection of the Thai architect Saengaroon Ratagasikorn, who studied in the US under Frank Lloyd Wright. He became fascinated with the design of farm implements: simple and beautiful yet still functional.

Siam Society The lovely garden belongs to the Siam Society, which also has an excellent library, highly recommended for anyone interested in Thai culture (call before visiting). The society also supports a gallery, holds lectures, organizes cultural trips throughout the· country and publishes interesting books on Thai culture and nature as well as the *Journal of the Siam Society*.

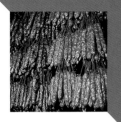

BANGKOK's best

51

Temples

Wat Phra Kaeo

THAI MEDITATION

Some Thai temples provide *Vipassana* or "insight" meditation sessions in English.
• World Fellowship of Buddhists (WFB) ⊠ 616 Benjasiri Park, Soi 24, Thanon Sukhumwit ☎ 0 2661 1284; www.wfb-hq.org
For free classes and forums in English every first Sunday of the month ⏰ 2–5.30
• International Buddhist Meditation Centre (BMC) ⊠ Mahachulalongkorn Buddhist University, Wat Mahathat, Thanon Naphratad ☎ 0 2222 6011

WAT BENJAMABORPIT

The "Marble Temple," the most recent of royal *wats*, is built from Carrara marble in a strange blend of traditional Thai temple architecture and European designs. The courtyard houses a collection of 53 Buddha images from all over Asia. It is an excellent place to watch religious festivals and moonlit processions. Unlike most other temples, monks don't go out seeking alms but are instead visited by merit-makers between 6 and 7am.

✚ E7 ⊠ Thanon Sri Ayudhaya and Thanon Rama V ⏰ Daily 8–5.30 🍴 Foodstalls 🚌 A/C bus 503 💷 Inexpensive

WAT BOWON NIWET
Built in 1829, this temple houses the Phra Phutthachinnasi, a very beautiful Buddha image molded around 1357. The temple is considered one of Bangkok's most important temples as King Rama UIV was chief abbot here before he ascended the throne. The current king was a monk here.
F7 Thanon Phra Sumen, Banglamphu 0 2281 2831 Daily 8–5 A/C bus 511 Free

WAT MAHATHAT
Wat Mahathat, one of the older shrines in Bangkok with a relic of Buddha, is home to Mahachulalongkorn University, an important Buddhist meditation and study center (► 52, panel). Some programs are organized for English-speaking visitors (ask at the Section 5 office for more information). On Sundays and Buddhist festivals a market is held on the precincts.
B8 Thanon Naphratad, near the Grand Palace 0 2222 6011 Daily 9–5 Foodstalls in market A/C bus 8, 12, 39 Maharat Free

WAT RATCHABOPIT
An unusual *wat*, built around 1869 by King Rama V, with very elaborate decoration. The mother-of-pearl doors and windows of the *bot* (chapel) are especially refined, and the hand-painted tiles clearly show European influence.
C8 Thanon Ratchabopit, off Thanon Atsadang 0 2222 3930 Daily 8 –5 A/C bus 507, 508 Tha Tian pier Free

WAT RATCHANADA
The strangest structure on this temple compound is Loha Prasad, or the Iron Monastery, a pink structure with weird metal spires. Bangkok's biggest amulet market is held daily on a nearby compound, and the stalls also sell other objects to ward off evil spirits.
D8 Off Thanon Maha Chai, opposite Wat Saket 0 2224 8807 Daily 8–5 Foodstalls A/C bus 511, 512 Free

WAT SUTHAT
Bangkok's tallest *viharn* (religious hall), at Wat Suthat, houses a 14th-century Buddha statue from Sukhothai surrounded by depictions of the Buddha's last 24 lives. The courtyard is filled with odd statues of scholars and sailors, brought as ballast in rice boats returning from China, while the doors of the *wat* are said to have been carved by King Rama II. In a former annual ceremony for the rice harvest men used to ride on the Giant Swing and try to grab a bag of silver coins attached to a pole; only the teak arch remains.
C8 Off Thanon Bamrung Muang, opposite the Giant Swing 0 2224 9845; www.watsuthat.org Daily 6–6 Foodstalls A/C bus 507, 508 Inexpensive

AMULETS (PHRA PHIM)

Amulets, often made by monks, depict images of Buddha, revered holy men, or famous monks. People choose their amulets very carefully as they are believed to have magical powers, the strength of which depends on the amulet's history or maker. Amulets come in various prices and with specific qualities: Some promise a happy love life or fertility, while others will protect against particular illnesses or bring good luck.

Wat Benjamaborpit

Markets

SHOPPING MAP

If you've come to Bangkok to shop till you drop in the markets, or if you're looking for something more specialized–that quaint little store selling hand-made papers, *satay* grills, or Chinese calendars–under no circumstances set off without Nancy Chandler's *Map of Bangkok*. The map, available from most English-language bookstores, covers Bangkok's main markets and shopping streets, highlighting the best, as well as the most unusual sights, known only to long-term residents. Her map is good for the new Suan Lum Night Market (► 55).

UP-COUNTRY MARKET

If the city gets to you, take the Chao Phraya express boat northward and get out at the last stop to visit the great market in Nonthaburi, the first town north of Bangkok. The trip itself is fun, passing rice barges, stilt-houses, and other common river sights. The market has a provincial feel and is known for its excellent fruits, especially the smelly durian, grown in local orchards (► 60, Klong Om).

BANG RAK MARKET

Although becoming increasingly confined, Bang Rak is one of the city's best fruit and vegetable markets, with produce fresh from the gardens and orchards of Thonburi across the river.

➕ E11 ✉ Thanon Charoen Krung (New Road), near Shangri-La Hotel
🕐 Daily 🍴 Foodstalls 🚃 Skytrain: Saphan Taksin 🛳 Tha Oriental pier

BANGLAMPHU MARKET

A huge market area with street vendors—selling all manner of travelers' essentials and extremely cheap clothing—as well as smarter department stores.

➕ C7 ✉ Around Thanon Chakkaphong, Thanon Phra Sumen, and Thanon Tanao, Thanon Khao San area 🕐 Daily morning–evening
🍴 Thanon Ram Buttri has several open-air Thai restaurants
🚌 A/C bus 506 🛳 Tha Phra Atit pier

PHAHURAT

Phahurat, the center of Bangkok's Indian community, has a series of cloth merchants, selling everything (bar Thai silk) from saris to curtain and furnishing fabrics.

➕ C9 ✉ Around Thanon Phahurat 🕐 Daily 🍴 Royal India Restaurant (► 69) 🚌 A/C bus 501, 507 🛳 Tha Saphan Phot pier

PRATHUNAM

A central market covering a large area and excellent for cheap clothes and fabrics. Wholesalers and exporters buy here, but also locals come here for casual wear, fresh produce and other essentials. There

Dried fish for sale in a street market

are plenty of seam-
stresses and tailors at
hand to make up your
outfit in a few hours.
Bargaining is a must.
🚩 H8 ✉ Intersection
Thanon Ratchaprarop and
Thanon Phetburi 🕐 Daily
9am–midnight 🍴 Foodstalls
🚊 Skytrain: Chitlom/
Phayathai 🚌 A/C bus 512

SUAN LUM NIGHT MARKET

Bangkok's newest
night market has more
than 3,700 stands, sell-
ing crafts, souvenirs
and some antiques,
offering a good alter-
native to those who
don't make it to the
Chatuchak weekend
market (➤ 48). Beer
gardens, restaurants
and a huge covered
food court with live
bands nightly.
🚩 H11 ✉ On the corner of
Thanon Rama IV and Thanon
Witthayu 🕐 Daily 3pm–
midnight 🍴 Foodstalls and
restaurants 🚇 Lumphini
🚌 A/C bus 13, 17, 76

THEWET FLOWER MARKET

Lovely, quiet flower
and plant market on a

Floating markets are one
of the city's most
appealing attractions

canal lined with beautiful old houses. The thousands
of exotic plants on offer here make it a must for plant
lovers. Take along *Gardening in Bangkok* by M. R. P.
Amranand, available from the Siam Society (➤ 50).
🚩 D6 ✉ Klong Phadung Krung Kasem, off Thanon Samsen 🕐 Daily
9–6 🍴 Foodstalls 🚌 A/C bus 505, 506 ⛴ Tha Thewet pier

THIEVES' MARKET (NAKORN KASEM)

This corner of Chinatown has its own distinct character. The narrow lanes are full of stores selling old and
new "antiques," as well as brass and musical instruments such as gongs and cooking equipment.
🚩 D9 ✉ Between Thanon Yaowarat, Thanon Boripat and Thanon
Chakkawat 🕐 Daily 8–8 🍴 Foodstalls 🚌 A/C bus 507, 508
⛴ Tha Saphan Phut

Architecture

CLASSIC THAI

Thai writer, Chami Jotisalikorn, argues that the Thai house is very "modern" as it conforms to the major dictums of the 20th-century architect Le Corbusier. He advocated that buildings should be raised on stilts with a roof garden used as a social space and a free flowing floor plan, all important elements of the traditional Thai house. Read more on Thai style in *Classic Thai: Interiors, Design, Architecture* by Chami Jotisalikorn, with photographs by Luca Invernizzi Tettoni (Asia Books, Bangkok 2003).

Baan Jim Thompson

In the Top 25
25 BAAN KAM THIENG (▶ 50)
20 WANG SUAN PAKKAD (▶ 45)

Until some twenty years ago, the roofs and *chedis* (pagodas) of temples dominated Bangkok's skyline, but today Western-style skyscrapers are a much more obvious feature. Most of the traditional Thai houses have now been converted into museums or into luxury residences. Both Thai and Western residents are now taking an interest in saving traditional houses and use Ayutthayan craftsmen to restore them. The Thai word for house is *baan*.

BAAN JIM THOMPSON
The house is as famous as the silk (▶ 43).

M.R. KUKRIT PRAMOJ MUSEUM
The house of the former prime minister, M.R. Kukrit Pramoj, who lived here until 1995, is one of the few places that gives an insight into traditional upper-class Thai life. Built in teak in Auyutthaya style, it has five beautiful rooms in a cluster. The interior is mostly as it was left in 1995. It includes modern air-conditioning, fine antiques and the *mai dat*, or Thai miniature trees, that were his passion.
✚ G11–12 ✉ 19 Soi Phra Phinit, Thanon Sathorn Tai ✉ 0 2286 8185 ⏰ Sat–Sun 10–5 💷 Inexpensive 🚊 Skytrain: Chong Nonsi 🚌 Bus 22, 62, 77, 162

THAI-STYLE HOTEL

To experience living in a traditional house, stay a few days at the Thai House Hotel, set in an orchard 14 miles (22km) north of Bangkok. A double room costs 1,700B; also offers trips to markets and Thai cookery classes.
✉ 32/4 Moo 8, Bongmuang Road, Bang Yai, Nonthaburi ☎ 0 2903 9611; email pipthaihouse@hotmail.com

PRASART MUSEUM
Prasart Vongsakul's (▶ 72) precious collection of Asian antiques (with artifacts dating from prehistoric times) is housed in a wonderful collection of traditional Thai houses set in beautifully kept tropical gardens. This museum is outside Bangkok but well worth the excursion if you love Thai architecture and arts. The Red Palace is an exquisite reproduction of the Tamnak Daeng, built in the Rama III period; the original is now in the national Museum (▶ 33).
✚ Off map ✉ 9 Soi 4A, Thanon Krungthepkritha, off Thanon Srinakarintora, Bang Kapi ☎ 0 2379 3601/7 ⏰ Fri–Sun 10–3 💷 Expensive 🚌 Bus 93 ❓ Reservation required

Places to Watch the City

BAIYOKE SKY HOTEL

The world's tallest hotel has an observation deck and restaurant on the 77th floor, with good-value buffet at lunchtimes.

🞦 H8 ⊠ 222 Thanon Ratchaphrarop, Prathunam ☎ 0 2656 3000; www.baiyokeskyhotel.com 🯀 Skytrain: Phaya Thai

ERAWAN SHRINE

This is a good place to see how important religion is for most Thais. No matter how westernized Thais look or behave, religion is still central to their lives, so here you'll see girls in Gucci or Marc Jacobs praying and offering flowers (► 46).

GOLDEN MOUNT

To view the grandeur of the Royal City of Rattanakosin, climb up the golden *chedi* on this 246-ft (75-m) high hill (► 37).

LUMPHINI PARK

Come to the park between 5 and 7am to view a healthier Bangkok, as Chinese practice *t'ai chi*, young Thais sweat at their aerobic classes, and joggers pound the track. In the late afternoon, rent a boat and go rowing across the lake and watch the often dramatic skyline (► 47).

TERRACE, ORIENTAL HOTEL

The most elegant place in Bangkok to enjoy an early evening drink. Watch the sun set over Thonburi and the river (► 41).

THANON PATPONG (PATPONG ROAD)

Thais and tourists flock to this area at night for *sanuk* (fun), shopping, eating and drinking in the bars, Also the nearby Thanon Silom becomes a long row of stalls and foodstalls (► 44)

VERTIGO

The Banyan Tree Hotel (► 86) has converted its helipad on the 61st floor into the highest al fresco bar-restaurant (656ft/200m) in the world. It is only open at night and the most spectacular place to see the city and *the* place to be seen. The slim-shape hotel also has spectacular views from its spa on the 57th floor

🞦 H11 ⊠ 21/100 South Sathorn Road ⊠ 0 2679 1200; www.banyantree.com 🯀 Skytrain: Sala Daeng 🚌 A/C bus 15, 67

WAT ARUN

Tackle the steep stairs up the central tower for a magnificent view over the Chao Phraya river (► 30); closed for restoration at time of writing.

Views from Wat Arun extend across the river

MORE BOOKS

• *Bangkok 8* (Corgi, 2004) by John Burdett. Crime novel with great insights into the city's underbelly and Thai Buddhism.

• *Jasmine Nights* (Penguin Books, London, 1995) by S. P. Somtow. Novel about a boy growing up on an estate off Sukhumwit and his adventures into the *klongs* (canals).

• *Bangkok* (Talisman, Singapore, 2002) by William Warren. Entertaining portrait of the city he has lived in and loved for 35 years.

• *Bangkok, Story of a City* (Little Brown, Boston, 1971) by Alec Waugh. History of the city.

57

Spas

Some enterprising spirits have sensed the rising stress levels arising from more frenetic and more hectic times and are opening spas where locals and visitors can be pampered. There are also traditional massage parlors on nearly every street corner where you can get anything from a one- or two-hour Thai massage to foot reflexology—even at Don Muang Airport: perfect preparation for a long-haul flight.

➕ Off map at K1 ✉ Terminal 1, Don Muang Airport ☎ 0 2535 4318

THAI MASSAGE

Thai curative massage was probably brought from India by Buddhist monks and, for centuries, it has been used to help alleviate various illnesses and ailments. The massage consists of controlled application of pressure by the masseur's hands to stimulate blood circulation. It also uses fresh herb bags rolled onto certain parts of the body. It is usually worth looking for the real thing—ask at your hotel for recommendations.

BANYAN TREE

The highest spa in Bangkok with great relaxing views, where the signature treatment is the Balinese Boreh with three hours of deep-tissue massage, herbal body wrap and a spicy rub.

➕ H11 ✉ Banyan Tree Hotel, 20th, 21st and 57th floors, 21/100 Thanon Sathorn Tai ☎ 0 2679 1200; www.banyantree.com ⏲ Daily 9am–10pm 🚇 Skytrain: Sala Daeng 🚌 A/C bus 15, 67 💷 Expensive

BEING SPA

Get pampered in the serene surroundings of this secluded spa.

➕ Off map at K10 ✉ 88 Sukhumwit 51, Klongton Neu, Wattana ☎ 0 2662 6171; www.beingspa.com ⏲ Daily 10–10 💷 Moderate–expensive

BUATHIP

This is an old-style parlor for traditional Thai and oil-with-herb massages.

➕ J9 ✉ 4/1–3 Sukhumwit Soi 5 ☎ 0 2251 2627 ⏲ Daily 10am–midnight 🚇 Skytrain: Nana 💷 Inexpensive

CELADON HOME SPA

You can have a spa in your hotel room. A neatly uniformed masseur transforms the room into a sanctuary with fresh flowers, mattress, slippers and incense

Massage as a healing art is an ancient tradition, but these days the term is more loosely applied

burners. The favorite package includes a rice and
lavender polish and a café latte scrub.
☎ 0 2643 1191; www.hotelthailand.com/spa/celadon ⏰ Daily
9am–10pm 💰 Moderate

DIVANA (MASSAGE AND SPA)

Get a massage on a bridge over the water lily pond in
this very peaceful and friendly spa, in a two-story
Thai house. Divana offers a wide range of treatments,
rubs, wraps and massages, all using their own chemi-
cal-free organic products which are available to buy
at reception.
➕ Off map at K10 ✉ 7 Sukhumvit 5 North Klongtoey, Wattana
☎ 0 2661 6784; www.divanaspa.com ⏰ Daily 7am–11pm, last
treatments at 9pm 🚉 Skytrain (BTS): Asoke 💰 Moderate

ORIENTAL HEALTH SPA

Traditional massages and just about every other body-
relaxing treat imaginable. The excellent "jet-lag
massage" is particularly recommended if you have
arrived in Bangkok on a long-haul flight (► 41).
➕ E11 ✉ Oriental Hotel, Thonburi side ☎ 0 2439 7613 ⏰ Daily
9am–10pm 🍴 Thai spa cuisine 🚉 Skytrain: Saphan Taksin 🚢 Tha
Oriental pier ♿ Very good 💰 Expensive

SPA BANGKOK

This spa is off the busy Silom Road. The most
popular treatments are the Aromatherapy Body
Massage and Salt Body Scrub. The staff are highly
trained and this spa is excellent value for money.
➕ G11 ✉ 15/11 Arnaruk Building, 2nd Floor, Silom Soi 3
☎ 0 2238 1850; www.spabangkok.com ⏰ Mon–Fri 1pm–10pm,
Sat–Sun noon–10pm 🚉 Skytrain: Sala Daeng 💰 Moderate

THE THERAPEUTIC AND HEALING MASSAGE COURSE (IN ENGLISH)

A first course teaches the ethics and rules of massage
and basic techniques for relieving fatigue and tension.
The second course goes into advanced techniques for
pain relief, muscular problems and nervous tension.
➕ B/C9 ✉ Wat Po Traditional Medical School, Wat Po, Thanon Sanam
Chai, Tha Tian pier ☎ 0 2221 2974 ⏰ Each course takes 30 hours
over 15 days, to be arranged with teacher 🚌 A/C bus 506, 507, 508,
512 🚢 Tha Tian pier

TRADITIONAL MEDICAL PRACTITIONERS' ASSOCIATION CENTER

One of the best and certainly the least expensive
places to experience a traditional massage is at this
center on the Wat Po grounds. They certainly know
what they are doing, and although it looks (and sometimes feels) a little painful to be pulled into all those
weird positions, the after-effect is heavenly.
➕ B/C9 ✉ Wat Po, Thanon Maha Rat ☎ 0 2221 2974 ⏰ Daily
10–6 🚌 A/C bus 506, 507, 508, 512 🚢 Tha Tian pier 💰 Inexpensive

HOME SPA

Most spas sell their own
products but some shops also
specialize in spa products. The
natural Simmons products
(www.simmonsnaturals.com)
and Thann (www.thann.info) are
based on aromatherapy and use
rice bran oil. Both are available
from Exotique Thai (► 77) at
the Emporium Shopping
Complex.

Klongs (Canals)

GETTING LOST

There is no proper map available of the Thonburi *klongs*. According to Bangkok-based author William Warren, a foreigner who asked for one from the government was told that such information was a "military secret." But, for more information, check *Bangkok's Waterways, An Explorer's Handbook* by William Warren (Asia Books, 1989).

BARGE PROGRAM

The Manohra is a 100-year-old restored rice barge that does excellent dinner cruises and occasionally also takes tours into the *klongs* or on the Chao Phraya river (✉ Bangkok Marriott Resort and Spa, Than Charoen Nakhon, Thonburi ☎ 0 2677 6240). As part of its cultural classes, the Oriental Hotel runs a wonderful tour of the klongs with a knowledgeable lecturer on board (☎ 0 2859 9000).

Traditional klong *life, with houses built on stilts*

DAMNOEN SADUAK FLOATING MARKET

This lively floating market (*talaat naam*) may only be a shadow of its former glory, but it still gives a good feel of what these floating markets used to be, especially if you arrive before 9am when the many package tours from Bangkok arrive. The 100-year old market has mainly boats selling souvenirs and fruits, but it is still possible to find traditional Thailand in the residential canals just beyond the market.

➕ Off map at A13 ✉ Klong Damnoen Saduak, Ratchaburi Province, 40 miles (65km) southwest of Bangkok ⏰ Daily 4am–noon 🍴 Foodstalls on boats 🚌 A/C bus 78, 996 from Thonburi Southern Bus Terminal to Klong Damnoen Saduak, then water-taxi or walk ❓ Bangkok Tourist Bureau organizes tours (☎ 0 2225 7612)

KLONG BANGKOK NOI

Once you have passed the Royal Barge Museum (➤ 26) and the little-visited Wat Suwannaram, there is a touch of the jungle between old crumbling *wats* and typical Thai teak houses.

➕ A–B7 🚤 Inexpensive canal taxis go up the *klong* from Tha Maha Rat pier, and long-tail boats leave from Chang Wang Luang pier. Private companies operate excursions to the Royal Barge Museum and farther up the *klong* from Chang pier

KLONG OM

A wonderful excursion through durian plantations, fruit orchards, little temples and grand river mansions. Recommended if you would like a feeling of rural Thailand.

➕ Off map at C1 ✉ Nonthaburi 🍴 Floating restaurant 🚤 Chao Phraya express boat to Nonthaburi, then long-tail boat up Klong Om. On Saturdays 8.30am–12.30pm Chao Phraya Express boats go from Tha Chang along Khlong Om. There are also daily tours from the River City pier (☎ 0 2266 9316)

KLONG SAN SAP

The fastest way to get across one of the most congested parts of the city, and undoubtedly the most adventurous and exotic. The urban *klong* scenery is an eye-opener, but the waters get quite smelly in the heat.

➕ D8–J9 ✉ From Golden Mount parallel to Thanon Bamrung Muang, Thanon Rama I, Thanon Ploenchit, and Thanon Sukhumwit 🚤 Long-tail boats operate eastward from Phanfa pier at the Golden Mount, past Jim Thompson's House

Festivals

What's On
See ▶ 4

ASALHA PUJA
The third most important Buddhist festival, marking the day of Lord Buddha's first sermon, usually in July and at the beginning of the three-month retreat (▶ panel). Thais gather at temples waiting for the moon to rise, then they follow the chanting monks three times around the *wat*, carrying flowers, incense and candles, which they then offer in front of the temple.

KITE FIGHTS
During breezy afternoons in March and April, Sanam Luang and Lumphini Park turn into colorful spectacles of magnificent kites. The huge "male" kites, or *chulas*, try to catch the smaller "females," or *pukpaos*, to the cheers of the public.

High spirits at the annual Songkran water-throwing festival, held in April

LOY KRATHONG
According to legend, a princess in Sukhothai made a small boat from a banana leaf to please her king; this has since become a rite of thanks to Mae Khongkha (Mother of Waters). On the night of the full moon in November, at the time of the floods, rivers and *klongs* are lit up with thousands of floating candles.

MAGA PUJA
Commemoration of the day 1,200 disciples gathered to hear Buddha preach, Thais go to *wats* to listen to sermons by the chief monk. When the moon rises they circle the *wat* as during Asalha Puja (February).

SONGKRAN
The water-throwing festival is the chance for every usually reserved Thai to let loose. Some water is sprinkled on friends to bless them, but strangers often get more than that. Expect to be completely soaked by midday, but who cares in the heat of April?

VISAKA PUJA
The holiest day of the Buddhist year is the day Lord Buddha was born, became enlightened and died. This is one of the more public festivals and ends with a candle-lit procession around *wats*. It is at its most solemn in Wat Benjamaborpit (▶ 52).

THREE-MONTH RETREAT

Tradition has it that farmers asked Buddha to keep all the monks in their *wats* for the three months after they planted out their rice, because otherwise the monks walked all over the young shoots when collecting their morning alms. Buddha took them seriously and there is still a three-month retreat period for monks (Khao Pansa), which starts with Asalha Puja and ends in October when people go to *wats* with new robes for the monks.

For Kids

COOLING DOWN

Most moderate and luxury hotels have swimming pools to cool you down, but not all are suitable for children. The best pools for youngsters are at the Shangri-La, the Peninsula and the Marriott Royal Garden Riverside 86). The Oriental has introduced a day-care center for children in residence. Alternatively, try ice skating at the World Trade Center (✉ 4 Thanon Ratchadamri ☎ 0 2255 9500 🕐 Daily 10am–8.30pm).

Up, up and away in Sanam Luang

THE BANGKOK DOLL FACTORY & MUSEUM

Khunying Tongkorn Chandevimol's private collection of dolls from her own factory and all over the world.

🔟 H8 ✉ Soi Ratchataphan (Soi Mo Leng), off Thanon Ratchaprarop Road ☎ 0 2245 3008 🕐 Mon–Sat 8–5 🚌 A/C bus 63 💰 Free

CHILDREN'S DISCOVERY CENTER

Set in Queen Sirikit Park, with its 12-acre (5-ha) botanical gardens, this museum aims to let children learn about science and nature through play.

🔟 J2/3 ✉ 4 Thanon Kamphaeng Phet, Chatuchak ☎ 0 2615 7333; www.bkkchildrenmuseum.com 🕐 Tue–Fri 9–6, Sat–Sun 10–7 🚌 A/C bus 510 🚇 Skytrain: Mo Chit 💰 Inexpensive

DUSIT ZOO (KHAO DIN WANA)

Includes rare species such as the Komodo dragon and the royal white elephants, sadly chained for most of the time. A circus is held at weekends 11am–2pm. Foodstalls, a playground and a boating lake.

🔟 E6 ✉ Thanon Rama V and Thanon Ratchawithi ☎ 0 2281 2000 🕐 Daily 9–5 🚌 A/C bus 510 ♿ Good 💰 Inexpensive

JAMBOREE

Corner of a huge shopping center dedicated to children. Indoor playground, video games, cars and creative activities at weekends. Good supervision.

🔟 Off map at J10 ✉ 3rd floor, The Emporium, beween Soi 22–24, Thanon Sukhumwit ☎ 0 2664 8000 🕐 Mon–Fri 10.30–10, Sat–Sun 10–10 🚇 Skytrain: Phrom Phong 🚌 A/C bus 502, 508, 511

QUEEN SAORABHA MEMORIAL INSTITUTE (SNAKE FARM)

Wide display of poisonous snakes, plus demonstrations of snake handling and venom milking.

🔟 G10 ✉ 1871 Thanon Phra Rama IV ☎ 0 2252 0161 🕐 Mon–Fri 8.30–4.30, Sat–Sun 8.30–noon 🚌 A/C bus 507 💰 Moderate

SAFARI WORLD

The world's largest zoo includes giraffes, lions, rhinos and monkeys, plus a marine park and bird area.

🔟 Off map at K1 ✉ 99 Thanon Ramindra, Minburi, 5.6 miles (9km) from city center ☎ 0 2518 1000; www.safariworld.com 🕐 Mon–Sun 9–5 🚌 27 Victory Monument–Minburi 💰 Expensive

BANGKOK
where to...

Thai

PRICES

Approximate prices for a meal for two excluding drinks:

$ = under 800B
$$ = 800–1800B
$$$ = more than 1800B

A TYPICAL THAI MEAL

Since the majority of Thais eat at street food stalls or at home, Thai restaurants in Bangkok are more oriented toward foreign visitors who may be unused to chillis. If you want your food red-hot, mention it when you order otherwise you will be disappointed. A meal usually consists of some appetizers or a spicy salad followed by at least one curry, a noodle dish, steramed rice and a soup. Thais eat with a spoon (right hand) and use a fork (left hand) to help the food onto the spoon. They take just one mouthful of a dish on their plate so as not to appear greedy, then move on to the next dish.

AROUND THE ORIENTAL HOTEL

HARMONIQUE ($$)

Old Chinese shophouse filled with antiques and fountains. Popular for its excellent Thai dishes.
✚ E11 ✉ 22 Soi Charoen Krung 34 ☎ 0 2237 8175 🕐 Mon–Sat 11am–10pm 🚌 A/C bus 501 ⛴ Tha Wat Muang Kai or Tha Oriental

SALATHIP ($$$)

Carefully prepared royal Thai cuisine in the romantic and elegant setting of a carved teak pavilion that overlooks the Chao Phraya river and lotus ponds.
✚ E11 ✉ Riverside, Shangri-La Hotel, 8 Soi Wat Suan Phu ☎ 0 2236 7777 🕐 Nightly 6.30–10.30 🚈 Skytrain: Saphan Taksin 🚌 A/C bus 504 ⛴ Tha Oriental or Shangri-La piers

SILOM/THANON SATORN

ANNA'S CAFÉ ($$)

Named after Anna in *The King and I*, this large, contemporary restaurant is the original of the five branches. On the menu are a few European ones. Extremely popular with young professionals and some movie stars.
✚ G11 ✉ 118 Soi Sala Daeng, off Thanon Silom ☎ 0 2632 0620 🕐 11–11 🚈 Skytrain: Sala Daeng 🚌 A/C bus 502, 504

BLUE ELEPHANT ($$$)

The Blue Elephant made its name outside Thailand first as a chain of stylish gourmet Thai restaurants; now they have their place in Bangkok as well. The restaurant and cooking school is set in a gorgeous colonial building. The menu offers a good mix of traditional royal cuisine, "Forgotten Recipes" and innovative Thai cuisine under "Our Chef's Creations."
✚ F12 ✉ Blue Elephant Building, 233 South Sathorn Road ☎ 0 2673 9353 🕐 11.30–2.30, 6.30–10.30 🚈 Skytrain: Surasak

BUSSARACUM ($$)

Long-time favorite for its royal Thai cuisine and classical, elegant décor. Minced pork and shrimp in egg-net wrapping was supposedly King Rama II's preferred appetizer. There is an excellent buffet lunch for less than 200B.
✚ G11 ✉ Sethiwan Building, off Thanon Convent ☎ 0 2266 6312 🕐 Lunch, dinner 🚈 Skytrain: Surasak

CELADON ($$–$$$)

One of Bangkok's most celebrated and beautiful restaurants: Inside it's minimalist Thai, outside there are lotus ponds and banana trees. The modern cuisine is just as spectacular, the roast duck curry is particularly good.
✚ H11 ✉ Sukhothai Hotel, 13/3 Thanon Satorn Tai ☎ 0 2344 8888; www.sukhothai.com 🕐 Lunch, dinner 🚈 Skytrain: Sala Daeng 🚌 A/C bus 505

SUKHUMWIT

AAO ($$–$$$)

This stunning modern restaurant and bar, in

orange and cream shades with lots of portholes and circles, is run by three sisters: Ae, Am and Oil. The food is excellent and can best be described as beautifully presented and inventive Thai cuisine.

➕ H10 ✉ 45/4–8 Soi LangSuan, Ploenchit Road ☎ 0 2254 5698 ⏱ Tue–Sun 11–10.30 🚆 Skytrain: Chitlom 🚌 A/C bus 501, 508

BAAN KHANITHA AND GALLERY ($$–$$$)

Award-winning restaurant. Both branches are in gorgeous converted villas with al fresco dining. The food is unique, the presentation is superb and the interiors are designed by owner, Khun Kanitha.

➕ J9/10 ✉ 349 Soi Ruam Ruedi, Thanon Ploenchit ☎ 0 2253 4638 Other branch ✉ 36/1 Sukhumwit 23, Soi Prasanmit ☎ 0 2258 4128 ⏱ Lunch, dinner 🚆 Skytrain: Ploen Chit 🚌 A/C bus 501, 508

LAICRAM ($$)

This great restaurant offers superior and authentic Thai dishes, such as a delicious seafood curry, or *Somtam* (spicy green papaya salad) at surprisingly good prices. The interior is pretty straightforward, but locals come here for the excellent food.

➕ Off map at K8 ✉ Soi 23 Thanon Sukhumwit ☎ 0 2204 1069 ⏱ 10–9 (until 3 on Sun) 🚆 Skytrain: Asoke 🚇 Sukhumwit

LEMON GRASS ($$)

This palm-shaded townhouse with a

distinctive Asian interior is an old favorite, and serves delicious and imaginative dishes with a touch of "royalty."

➕ Off map at K10 ✉ 5/1 Soi Sukhumwit 24 ☎ 0 2258 8637 ⏱ 11–2, 6–11 🚆 Skytrain: Phrom Phong 🚌 A/C bus 501, 508, 511, 513

THE SPICE MARKET ($$–$$$)

The interior looks slightly dated but the food is still top notch at this friendly restaurant. From the soft shell crab curry or Pad Thai (Thai noodles) to the home-style ice creams of coconut, tamarind or green tea. Everything tastes simply delicious.

➕ H9 ✉ Four Seasons Bangkok, 155 Thanon Ratchadamri ☎ 0 2251 6127; www.fourseasons.com ⏱ Lunch, dinner 🚆 Skytrain: Ratchadamri 🚌 A/C bus 505

VIENTIANE KITCHEN ($$)

This rather ramshackle restaurant serves some of the most exciting food in town, mainly from Isaan province and Laos. The flavors of this food are complex, intriguing and extremely delicious; really spicy if you want it to be. The service is peaceful and friendly, making the dining experience utterly pleasing. A live band plays traditional music, and with the open air atmosphere really makes for a special evening.

➕ Off map at K10 ✉ 8 Thanon Sukhumwit Soi 36 ☎ 0 2258 6171 ⏱ 11–midnight 🚆 Skytrain: Thong Lo

FOOD COURTS

Thais love eating their snacks or meals at food courts, usually located around shopping malls or office areas. The atmosphere is great sitting outside at night, while on a hot day the air-conditioned environment is a tempting option (especially if you're on a shopping mission). Venues vary from the basic snack-type place found close to supermarkets to trendy upmarket food courts like the stylish Loft (▶ below). Food courts are a great way to sample a range of Thai dishes and flavors at small prices. Every stand or mini kitchen has its specialties, and ingredients are always fresh. You usually buy a set of vouchers and then pay for food in vouchers.

THE LOFT

This trendy food court in a black minimalist interior with great lighting, has a plastic card paying system instead of the usual vouchers. Food stands sell traditional Thai dishes, Vietnamese and Northern Thai as well as a few classy Western-style deserts and everything tastes wonderful. It is 50 percent more expensive than the standard food court on the first floor, but definitely worth a visit.

➕ H9 ✉ Central Department Store, Thanon Ploenchit ☎ No phone ⏱ 10–10 🚆 Skytrain: Chitlom 🚌 A/C bus 501, 508

Thai Food & Culture

FOOD CULTURE

If you really want to know about Thai food try a cookery class, which usually ends with you eating what you have prepared. The chefs at the Oriental Hotel (➤ 41) teach people how to cook the refined Thai dishes served at their restaurants, in a morning class or session of five mornings. The Landmark Hotel also runs good morning and afternoon classes (✉ Thanon Sukhumwit between Sois 6 and 8 ☎ 0 2254 0404 🚊 Skytrain: Nana). The Blue Elephant School of Cooking (➤ 64; ☎ 0 2673 9353; www.blueelephant. com/school) does very good state-of-the-art cooking classes. If you want to get really immersed go and stay at the Thai House (➤ 56, panel) for a four-day course with trips to local markets as well as cooking classes in peaceful surroundings.

BAAN THAI ($$)

Excellent Thai cuisine accompanied by classical Thai dancing between 8.45–10.45.

✚ Off map at K10 ✉ 7 Soi Sukhumwit 32 ☎ 0 2258 5403 🕒 Dinner 7–11 🚊 Skytrain: Thong Lo 🚌 A/C bus 501, 508, 511

HORIZON I & II ($$)

Regular night cruises on the Chao Phraya. Excellent international buffet with fresh salads, broiled fish and meats and very good desserts.

✚ E12 ✉ Shangri-La Hotel, 89 Soi Wat Sun Plu, Bangrak ☎ 0 2236 7777 🚊 Skytrain: Saphan Takson 🚢 Tha Shangri-La pier

LOY NAVA ($$–$$$)

Dinner is served on this teak rice barge full of charm and history. There's a good show while cruising.

✚ E11 ✉ Tha Oriental Pier ☎ 0 2437 7329/4932; www.loynava.com 🕒 Departs 6pm and 8pm 🚢 from Tha Oriental pier

MANOHRA ($$$)

Along with its sister boat, the *Manohra Moon*, this 100-year-old converted rice barge is now home to an elegant floating restaurant and cocktail bar. Thai food is served as you cruise past the illuminated Wat Arun and Grand Palace.

✚ Off map at C13 ✉ Marriott Royal Garden Riverside, 257/1–3 Thanon Charoen Nakorn (at Krung Thep Bridge) ☎ 0 2677 6240 🕒 Departs every evening from the hotel's pier at 7.30, returning at 10 🚌 Free shuttle boat from Oriental Hotel and River City Shopping Complex

SALA RIM NAAM ($$$)

Another Bangkok institution, the Rim Naam stages daily performances by dancers from the Fine Arts School. The food sometimes takes second place to the spectacle.

✚ E11 ✉ Thonburi side of the Oriental Hotel (48 Soi Oriental) ☎ 0 2437 2918 🕒 Dinner (shows at 7 and 8.30pm) 🚊 Skytrain: Saphan Taksin 🚢 Tha Oriental

SILOM VILLAGE ($$)

Huge semi-outdoor restaurant surrounded by craft and textile stores. Wide selection of fresh seafood to choose from, as well as other Thai dishes. Children are welcome. Good show every night of traditional Thai dances and music.

✚ F11 ✉ 286 Thanon Silom ☎ 0 2622 0080 🕒 10am–11pm 🚊 Skytrain: Chong Nonsi 🚌 A/C bus 502, 504, 505

SUPATRA RIVER HOUSE ($$)

Beautifully converted teak house on the river with good Thai dishes. The house has a small crafts museum and demonstrations of food sculpting. Every Friday and Saturday, see interpretations of classic Thai stories by Patravadi theater group (➤ 83).

✚ B9 ✉ 266 Soi Wat Rakang, Thanon Arumamarin, Thonburi ☎ 0 2411 0305 🕒 Dinner shows Fri–Sat 8.30–9pm 🚢 Cross-river ferry from Tha Chang to Tha Wat Rakang

Seafood

DAIRY QUEEN ($$)

This fine Thai-style seafood restaurant slightly out of town, enjoys a wonderful location on the Chao Phraya River. Thais love this restaurant, which says something about the quality of the food, so be sure to reserve ahead. Also offers dining cruises to the Grand Palace.

➕ Off map to north ✉ next to Saphan (bridge) Param Gau on Rattanathibet Road, 25 mins drive on expressway (no public transport) ☎ 0 2921 8670 🕙 Lunch, dinner

JEY HOY ($)

This popular al fresco restaurant has seafood, at reasonable prices, as a specialty. Early in the evening it is packed with Thai families who come for the house favorites such as stir-fried crab and fish curry.

➕ F7 ✉ Soi 2 Thanon Samsen, Banglamphu ☎ No phone 🕙 6pm–midnight 🚌 A/C bus 506 ⛴ Tha Phra Athit

KALOANG HOME KITCHEN ($$)

Very simple but delightful seafood restaurant in a small *soi* with wooden houses overlooking the Chao Phraya river and the Royal Yacht pier, next to the Queen's childhood home. The food is superb, and great value; the views are magnificent.

➕ C6 ✉ 2 Thanon Sri Ayudhaya, Dusit (at the end of Thanon Sri Ayudhay 2, behind the National Library) ☎ 0 2281 9228 🕙 11am–11pm 🚌 A/C bus 505 ⛴ Thai Thewet pier

PIERSIDE SEAFOOD RESTAURANT ($$)

Choose from the fresh seafood counter or order from the menu, which includes great crab in yellow curry and butter-baked Phuket lobsters. At night enjoy the great river views from the terrace or dine inside among lots of teak wood and gold leaf.

➕ E11 ✉ Ground level, River City Shopping Complex, 23 Soi Captain Bush ☎ 0 2237 0077 🕙 Lunch, dinner ⛴ Tha River City pier

SEAFOOD MARKET ($$–$$$)

This restaurant's slogan is: "If it swims we have it!" And there is more—an unbelievable selection of the freshest seafood, vegetables and fruit, all sold by weight and prepared in the style of your choosing, or as your food consultant (these are more than waiters) recommends.

➕ K10 ✉ 89 Soi Sukhumwit 24 ☎ 0 2261 2529 🕙 11am–midnight 🚈 Skytrain: Phrom Phong 🚌 A/C bus 501, 508, 511

YOK YOR ($$)

Popular Thai-style seafood restaurant on the banks of the Chao Phraya, with Thai, Chinese, Japanese and European dishes and live pop music. The specialty is a fiery *haw mok*, or fish curry. An inexpensive evening cruise leaves daily at 8pm.

➕ C6 ✉ 4 Thanon Wisut Kasat, Thonburi ☎ 0 2437 1121 🕙 10am–11.30pm 🚌 A/C bus 506 ⛴ Wisuthi pier

THE LOVE OF FOOD

Thais love eating, as is obvious from the wide selection of restaurants in Bangkok—it is claimed that there are over 50,000, and that's not counting the foodstalls that set up on every street and the food boats along the canals. You won't go hungry, that's for sure. But if your heart is set on one particular restaurant, be sure to make a reservation—others might feel the same way about it.

All Asian

CHINESE CUISINE

If you want to cool your palate down after the often fiery Thai food, try one of the more authentic Chinese restaurants. Most Chinese in Bangkok come from the Guangdong and Yunnan provinces, well known for their delicious cuisine. Some of the best food can be sampled at the hundreds of inexpensive street stalls in Chinatown, or in the more expensive Chinese restaurants in hotels–there are very few Chinese restaurants in the middle price range.

CHINESE

CAFÉ CHINOIS ($$)

This modern and very casual Chinese restaurant with fresh and inventive dishes, makes an excellent lunch stop while shopping. The fried shrimp with cream salad in *taro* nest is superb.

✚ Off map at K10 ✉ Emporium Shopping Complex, 2nd floor, Thanon Sukhumvit at Soi 24 ☎ 0 2664 8844 ◷ 10.30–10 🚇 Skytrain: Phrom Phong 🚌 A/C bus 508, 511

CHINA HOUSE ($$$)

The best of classic Cantonese and regional Chinese cuisine served in an elegant, beautifully restored private residence outside the Oriental Hotel. Dim sum is available at lunchtime.

✚ E11 ✉ Oriental Hotel, 48 Soi Oriental ☎ 0 2659 9000 ◷ Lunch, dinner 🚇 Skytrain: Saphan Taksin 🚢 Tha Oriental pier

MEI JIANG ($$$)

Stunning Chinese restaurant serving superb and refined Cantonese dishes, in an elegant art-deco interior. Great views of Bangkok at night.

✚ D12 ✉ Peninsula Hotel, 333 Thanon Charoen Nakorn ☎ 0 2861 2888 ◷ Lunch, dinner 🚇 Skytrain: Saphan Taksin (then shuttle boat to hotel)

SHANGARILA ($–$$)

Well-established Cantonese restaurant in the heart of Chinatown, serving all the classic dishes, including a good Peking duck, to a mainly Chinese clientele.

✚ E9 ✉ 206 Thanon Yaowarat, Chinatown ☎ 0 2235 7493 ◷ 11–10 🚌 A/C bus 501 🚢 Tha Ratchawong pier

WHITE ORCHID HOTEL ($$)

A great place for a dim sum lunch when you are in Chinatown.

✚ D9 ✉ 490–421 Thanon Yaowarat ☎ 0 2226 0026 ◷ 10.30am–11pm 🚢 Tha Ratchawong pier

INDIAN

HIMALI CHA CHA ($$)

Cha Cha started off as cook to Lord Mountbatten when he was the last British Viceroy in India. He went on to work for Indian ambassadors around the world, before he and his family settled in Bangkok. Specialties include Mughal Muslim, vegetarian and northern Indian dishes, all served in a quaintly charming, if old-fashioned, Indian interior.

✚ E11 ✉ 1229/11 Thanon Charoen Krung (New Road), corner of Thanon Surawong ☎ 0 2235 1569 ◷ Lunch, dinner 🚌 A/C bus 502, 505 🚢 Tha Oriental pier

RANG MAHAL ($$)

Some of the finest South Indian food in town is served in pleasant and elegant surroundings, and accompanied by Indian classical music.

✚ Off map at K10 ✉ Rooftop of the Rembrandt Hotel, 19 Sukhumvit Soi 18 ☎ 0 2261 7100 ◷ 11–11 🚇 Skytrain: Asoke 🚌 A/C bus 501, 508, 511, 513

ROYAL INDIA ($–$$)

Another delightful but hard-to-find place (squeezed between Chinatown and Phahurat), which is renowned for its well-prepared north Indian cuisine. Vegetarians will find a larger selection of vegetable dishes here than in most other Bangkok restaurants.

🚹 C/D9 ✉ 392/1 Thanon Chakpetch—small *soi* south of Soi Wanit 1 (Sampeng Lane) ☎ 0 2221 6565 ⏰ 10–10 🚢 Tha Saphan Phut

JAPANESE

MATOI CHAYA ($)

An old fashioned sushi bar in this street with Japanese bars and sex clubs, that sells great cheap sushi, mainly to Japanese.

🚹 G11 ✉ 19/16–17 Soi Thaniya ☎ 0 2632 7853 ⏰ Lunch, dinner 🚉 Skytrain: Sala Daeng

NIPPON TEI ($$$)

Reputedly one of the best Japanese restaurants in town and popular with Japanese visitors. A great selection of sashimi and sushi, and excellent Kobe beef in its own hot pot, plus great seafood dishes.

🚹 H9–10 ✉ 161 Thai Obayashi Building, B/F Thanon Ratchadamri ☎ 0 2252 9438 ⏰ Lunch, dinner 🚉 Skytrain: Ratchadamri 🚌 A/C bus 504, 505

VIETNAMESE

SWEET BASIL ($$)

Exquisite Vietnamese/ Thai cuisine served in an old house in this quiet alley oozing with the atmosphere of an older Bangkok.

🚹 F12 ✉ 1 Thanon Sirivieng, off Soi Pramuan, Silom ☎ 0 2238 3088 ⏰ Lunch, dinner 🚉 Skytrain: Surasak

FUSION

CONFUSION ($$)

Small and relaxed restaurant, with dark wooden furniture, which serves a fushion cuisine with—as they claim—the best of the East, mainly Thailand and the West. For example there is "the East meets West Spice Explosion" featuring cajun chicken with coconut served with Thai jasmine rice or "Kiwi Spring" a dish of New Zealand lamb marinated in Thai red curry. Lots of cocktails, too.

🚹 Off map at K10 ✉ 18/6 Sukhumvit Soi 23 ☎ 0 9121 0633; www.thaiconfusion.com ⏰ 6pm–11pm 🚉 Skytrain: Asoke 🚇 Sukhumvit

EAT ME ($$)

Very exciting and buzzing restaurant on several floors and outside terraces. The look is modern Asian, the music is great, waiters are friendly and the food is some of Bangkok's finest. The menu changes often but a few favorites remain such as crab and pomelo salad, linguine with spicy soft shell crab and the sticky date pudding with hot butterscotch.

🚹 G11 ✉ Soi Pipat 2, off Convent Road. Silom ☎ 0 2238 0931 ⏰ 6pm–1am 🚉 Skytrain: Sala Daeng

VEGETARIAN OPTIONS

Vegetarians who visit Bangkok during the annual Vegetarian Festival (September to October) will find Chinatown awash with foodstalls serving Thai and Chinese vegetarian dishes. At other times of the year a choice of fresh vegetable dishes is served at most Indian and Thai restaurants. Most dishes can be made vegetarian, just mention you are *tann jay*. The city's best vegetarian restaurant is The Whole Earth (✉ 93/3 Soi Lang Suan, off Thanon Ploenchit ☎ 0 2252 5574). Check the website www.ivu.org/tvu for vegetaria and vegetarian-friendly restaurants in Bangkok. Govinda (✉ Soi 22 Thanon Sukhumvit ☎ 0 2663 4970) was voted the city's best Italian vegetarian restaurant.

All Western

HIGH TEA

The Chinese claim that hot tea is the best way to cool down and to recover from the heat. English tea is something of an institution in Bangkok. The traditional place to take it is the Author's Lounge in the Oriental Hotel (➤ 41), but the grand lobbies of the Four Seasons (➤ 86), and the Shangri-La Hotel, only on Sundays, (✉ 89 Soi Wat Suan Phlu, Thanon Charoen Krung ☎ 0 2236 7777) and Peninsula (➤ 86) also offer splendid tea-time buffets of pastries, sandwiches, Thai sweets and pies, accompanied by uplifting classical music. The Café Oriental at the Emporium (➤ 76) also has a good selection.

AMERICAN

BOURBON STREET ($$)

Charming Cajun restaurant with New Orleans/Southern-style specials such as jambalaya, blackened red fish and pecan pie. Also has an American-style bar.
✚ Off map at K10 ✉ 29/4–6 Washington Square, Soi Sukhumvit 22 ☎ 0 2259 0328 🕐 Breakfast, lunch, dinner 🚉 Skytrain: Phrom Phong or Asote 🚌 A/C bus 501, 508

INTERNATIONAL

LE CAFÉ SIAM ($$)

An elegant restaurant in a charming house, where all the art and furniture is also for sale. The excellent food is half Thai, half French, and worth the search. They will even fax you a map.
✚ J12 ✉ 4 Soi Sriakson, off Thanon Chuea Phloeng, off Thanon Rama IV ☎ 0 2671 0031 🕐 Lunch, dinner 🚉 Bonkai 🚌 A/C bus 507

CRÊPES & CO. ($)

This is Bangkok's first creperie in a beautiful Thai villa set in an exotic garden. The panckes are delicious and hugely popular, but on offer is also a wider selection of salads and dishes covering the entire Mediterranean region. Great brunch.
✚ K10 ✉ 18/1 Sukhumvit Soi 12 ☎ 0 2653 3990 🕐 9am–midnight 🚉 Skytrain: Asoke

THE MADISON ($$$)

The Madison has an inventive Manhattan-style menu, with Black Angus Argentinian beef as well as fresh seafood. There is an excellent wine list and a variety of malt whiskey. Dinner is more expensive, but worth it. The interior design blends Western and Eastern.
✚ H9 ✉ Regent Hotel, 155 Thanon Ratchadamri ☎ 0 2251 6127 🕐 Lunch, dinner, Sat–Sun dinner only 🚉 Skytrain: Ratchadamri 🚌 A/C bus 504, 505

RICKY'S COFFEE SHOP ($)

Attractive Chinese shophouse converted into a popular café with fresh juices, breakfasts, good coffee and vegetarian dishes.
✚ C7 ✉ 22 Thanon Phra Athit, Banglamphu ☎ 0 2846 3011 🕐 Mon–Sat 8am–9pm 🚌 A/C bus 506 ⛴ Tha Phra Athit pier

VERTIGO ($$)

The highest al fresco restaurant in the world serves excellent Mediterranean tapas as well as grilled lobster, fish and meats that are as good as the view. (➤ 57)

FRENCH

LE BANYAN ($$$)

Distinctive French restaurant in an old Bangkok house decorated with local furnishings and objets d'art. The house specialty is a traditional pressed duck (for two), and many dishes show Thai influences.
✚ J10 ✉ 59 Soi Sukhumvit 8 ☎ 0 2253 5556 🕐 Mon–Sat 6.30–9.30 🚉 Skytrain: Nana 🚌 A/C bus 501, 508

LYON ($$–$$$)

Award-winning honest home-style French cuisine served in an elegant villa. Specials are duck in orange sauce and *coq au vin*.

✚ J10 ⊠ 33/2 Corner of Soi Ruam Rudee 2, Thanon Ploenchit ☎ 0 2253 8141 ⏱ Mon–Sat lunch, dinner ☒ Skytrain: Ploenchit ⛴ A/C bus 501, 508

LE NORMANDIE ($$$)

For a formal, definitively elegant dining experience, come to Le Normandie (you'll need a reservation). Choice of exquisite à la carte dishes, good-value *menu dégustation*, impeccable service and stunning panoramic views.

✚ E11 ⊠ Top floor of Oriental Hotel, 48 Soi Oriental ☎ 0 2659 9000 ⏱ Lunch, dinner ☒ Skytrain: Saphan Taksin ⛴ Tha Oriental pier

ITALIAN

ANGELINI ($$$)

This stunning restaurant, set over three floors, is one of Bangkok's places to be seen. The food is regional Italian. A live band at night draws a crowd.

✚ E11 ⊠ Shangri-La, 89 Soi Wat Suan Plu, off Thanon Charoen Krung ☎ 0 2236 7777 ⏱ Lunch, dinner ☒ Skytrain: Saphan Taksin ⛴ Tha Shangri-La pier

LA BUCA ($$)

There is no menu, only the rather eccentric chef, Oreste, who tells you what he has cooking. This is a very pleasant place serving delicious Italian dishes, made with the best ingredients, often imported from Italy.

✚ J9 ⊠ 220/4 Sukhumwit Soi 1, Wattana ☎ 0 2253 3190 ⏱ 6.30am–11pm ☒ Skytrain: Ploenchit or Nana ⛴ A/C bus 501, 508

ZANOTTI ($$–$$$)

Super-trendy Italian restaurant with great food including house specialties such as beef fillet in rock salt and rocket salad with hot octopus. There is an excellent wine list too, but be sure to make reservations.

✚ G11 ⊠ 21/2 Sala Daeng Colonnade Building, Soi Sala Daeng ☎ 0 2636 0002 ⏱ Lunch, dinner ☒ Skytrain: Sala Daeng ⛴ A/C bus 502, 504, 505

ZANZIBAR ($$)

Very friendly Thai/Italian restaurant in a three-floor house from 1920. The food is excellent— especially the seafood pastas. Reservations.

✚ J9 ⊠ 139 Soi Sukhumwit 11 ☎ 0 2651 2700 ⏱ 11–2, 5.30–10 (also until 2am Fri, Sat) ☒ Skytrain: Nana ⛴ A/C bus 501, 508

MIDDLE EASTERN

NASER EL-MASRY ($–$$)

An Egyptian mirror palace in Bangkok's "Little Arabia." Great for broiled meats, stuffed vegetables, salads and fruit juices.

✚ E11 ⊠ 4/6 North Nana (Soi 3), Sukhumwit ☎ 0 2253 5582 ⏱ Breakfast, lunch, dinner ☒ Skytrain: Nana ⛴ A/C bus 501, 508

BUFFET MEALS

Some of the best Western food is to be found at hotels, but it tends to be expensive. Travelers on a tighter budget should instead check out the better-value lunch and dinner buffets. Sunday brunch (11–3) at the Sukhothai Hotel's Colonnade Restaurant, to the accompaniment of a jazz combo, is an absolute favorite with expats (► 86; make reservations well in advance). Le Meridien President (⊠ 971 Thanon Ploenchit (☎ 0 2253 0444)) has a popular lunch and dinner buffet with both Thai and French or Italian dishes. The Oriental Hotel's alfresco buffet is more expensive, but the riverside setting alone makes it worth while (► 41). For the best view, try the lunch buffet on the 78th floor of the Baiyoke Sky Hotel (► 57) or the dim sum lunch-buffet at the Bai Yun, 53rd floor of the Banyan Tree Hotel (► 86) .

Antiques

Most smart antiques shops are on the fourth floor of the River City Shopping Complex (✉ 23 Thanon Yotha, off Thanon Sri Phraya ☎ 0 2237 0077 ⛴ Tha Sri Phraya pier). The place for reasonably priced antiques is the Chatachuk Weekend Market (➤ 48), particularly in section 1.

ACALA

Gorgeous Tibetan antiques such as lacquer cupboards with flowers and bright rugs, as well as other unusual objects.
✚ E11 ✉ Room 312, River City Shopping Complex, 23 Thanon Yotha, off Thanon Sri Phraya ☎ 0 2237 0077 ext. 312; www.acala.com ⛴ Tha Sri Phraya pier

THE FINE ARTS THE HEIGHT

Beautiful store with miniature wooden boats (made to order), 19th-century silks and costumes and other textiles from Southeast Asia, collected by the knowledgeable Ms Wallee Padungsinseth.
✚ E11 ✉ Rooms 354 and 452–4, River City Shopping Complex, 23 Thanon Yotha, off Thanon Sri Phraya ☎ 0 2237 0077/8 ext. 354/452/554 🚌 Bus 36, 93 ⛴ Tha Sri Phraya pier

KUNTA

Small shop with exquisite Buddhas, amulets and small objects from Thailand and Cambodia.
✚ H9 ✉ Four Seasons Bangkok, 155 Thanon Ratchadamri ☎ 0 2651 9049 🚇 Skytrain: Ratchadamri 🚌 A/C bus 504, 505

THAI CUSTOMS AND ANTIQUES

Fakes are particularly well made in Thailand and are sometimes sold as genuine antiques. To protect yourself, buy from a reputable shop. Antiques and Buddha images cannot be exported without a license, which can be obtained from the Fine Arts Department at the National Museum (✉ Thanon Naphratad ☎ 0 2221 4817). Some antiques stores will arrange the paperwork for you. Applications, submitted with two photographs of the object and a photocopy of your passport, usually take about five days to be processed.

L'ARCADIA

Small store with well-priced antique furniture and carved teak architectural ornaments, mainly from Thailand and Myanmar (Burma).
✚ Off map at K10 ✉ 12/2 Soi Sukhumvit 23 ☎ 0 2259 9595 🚇 Skytrain: Asoke 🚇 Sukhumvit

LEK GALLERY ART

This huge gallery specializes in Myanmar and Thai antiques, but it also features a stunning collection of old Japanese tapestries.
✚ E11 ✉ 1275–1277 Thanon Charoen Krung ☎ 0 2235 0109 🚇 Skytrain: Saphan Taksin ⛴ Tha Sri Oriental pier

NEOLD

As the name suggests this wonderful shop, owned by one of Thailand's top antique dealers and designers, specializes in combining the new with the old. High quality antiques, baskets, lacquerware, tapestries and furniture. There is another branch at the Four Seasons Hotel (➤ 86).
✚ F11 ✉ 149/2–3 Thanon Surawong ☎ 0 2235 8352 🚇 Skytrain: Sala Daeng

OLD MAPS AND PRINTS

Browse among old maps of Siam and South Asia, or look for wonderful prints. The knowledgeable owner, Joerg Kohler, can tell you all about them.
✚ E11 ✉ 4th floor, River City Shopping Complex, 23 Thanon Yotha, of Thanon Sri Phraya ☎ 0 2237 0077 🚌 Bus 36, 94 ⛴ Tha Sri Phraya pier

Gems & Jewelry

ANONG GALLERY
Impressive and unusual modern jewelry inspired by classic Thai and Buddhist designs.
✚ H9 ✉ 2nd floor, Peninsula Plaza, 153 Thanon Ratchadamri ☎ 0 2253 9772 🚇 Skytrain: Ratchadamri 🚌 A/C bus 504, 505

BUALAAD
Contemporary jewelry inspired by traditional designs, plus a wonderful collection of stones.
✚ H9 ✉ 106–7 Peninsula Plaza, 153 Thanon Ratchadamri ☎ 0 2253 9790 🚇 Skytrain: Ratchadamari 🚌 A/C bus 504, 505

FRANK'S JEWELRY CREATION
Ritzy jeweler to both Thai and international stars, with some of the most extravagant jewels. Prices are equally sky-high, but Frank will replicate any piece of jewelry.
✚ H9 ✉ Shop no 104, Peninsula Plaza, 153 Thanon Ratchadamri ☎ 0 2254 0764 🕐 Mon–Sat 10–6 🚇 Skytrain: Ratchadamari 🚌 A/C bus 504, 505

JOHNNY'S GEMS
One of the city's oldest jewelry emporiums. A selection for all budgets.
✚ D9 ✉ 199 Thanon Fueng Nakorn, Chinatown ☎ 0 2224 4065 ☎ Telephone for a free shuttle from your hotel

LOTUS ARTS DE VIVRE
Elegant and stylish stores with exquisite new and old jewelry and objets d'art from all over Asia. Suitably expensive.
✉ Branches at the Four Seasons and Sukhothai hotels (➤ 86), and at the Oriental (➤ 41)

SIPSONG PANNA SILVER (BANGKOK)
The Bangkok branch of a major antique silver dealer in Chiang Mai, this shop has an excellent collection of old silver, and particularly tribal and ethnic jewelry from several countries in mainland Southeast Asia. Also trades at Chatuchak Weekend Market (➤ 48).
✚ E11 ✉ 310 River City Shopping Complex, 23 Thanon Yotha, off Thanon Sri Phraya ☎ 0 2237 0077 ext. 310 ⛴ Tha Sri Phraya pier

TABTIM THAI
Mrs Yupha Steiner creates unique and stunning necklaces, earrings and other jewelry using semi-precious stones. Also at the Pink Poodle Four Seasons Hotel (➤ 86).
✚ E11 ✉ Author's Lounge at Oriental Hotel ☎ 0 2236 0400 ext. 3357 🚇 Skytrain: Saphan Taksin ⛴ Tha Orieintal pier

UTHAI'S GEMS
Very reliable jeweler with more conservative designs at good prices, known for its excellent custom work.
✚ J9 ✉ 28/7 Soi Ruam Ruedi, off Thanon Ploenchit ☎ 0 2253 8582 🚇 Skytrain: Ploen Chit 🚌 A/C bus 501, 508

YVES JOAILLIER
Yves Bernardeau's designs are often inspired by ancient jewels from the Mediterranean.
✚ H11 ✉ 3rd floor, Charn Issara Tower, Thanon Rama IV ☎ 0 2233 3292 🚇 Skytrain: Sala Daeng 🚌 A/C bus 507

BEWARE OF TOUTS!
Touts hang around all of Bangkok's main shopping areas, and for the unsuspecting shopper they mean trouble. Shop around before buying and remember that it is quite acceptable to bargain, even in more elegant stores. For an insight into the gem market, read John Hoskin's entertaining *Buyer's Guide to Thai Gems* (Asia Books, Bangkok, 1988). Locals are often happiest to recommend jewelers in hotel shopping arcades for their reliability. The Jewel Fest Club was established by the Tourism Authority of Thailand to combat gem fraud. Find out more at www.tat.or.th/do/jewel.htm

Silk & Fabrics

THAI SILK

The tradition of silk-making goes back hundreds of years in Thailand, but by the early 20th century Thais preferred less expensive imported fabrics and the industry went into decline. Old skills were being lost when Jim Thompson (➤ 43) discovered a few silk-weavers near his house, which gave him the idea of reviving the business. Jim Thompson's Thai Silk Company Ltd was founded in 1948 and was well reviewed in *Vogue*. Two years later he was commissioned to make the costumes for the Broadway production of *The King and I* and his success was assured. He is now referred to as the "King of Thai Silk."

ALTA MODA

Thai silk is beautiful but not practical for casual wear, so head here for a wide selection of other fabrics, from plain cotton to designer fabrics from Ungaro or Versace.
➕ Off map at K10 ✉ 31st floor, Emporium Shopping Complex ☎ 0 2255 9533 🚊 Skytrain: Phrom Phong 🚌 A/C bus 501, 508, 511

ANITA THAI SILK

Recommended by expatriates as the place to find reasonably priced and good-quality silk. There is a wide selection of fabrics, plus men's shirts and neckties.
➕ F11 ✉ 294/4–5 Thanon Silom ☎ 0 234 2481; anitasilk.com 🕐 Mon–Sat 8–6 🚊 Skytrain: Sala Daeng 🚌 A/C bus 502, 504, 505

DESIGN THAI

Three floors of silk fabrics, clothes and accessories, with furnishing fabrics, silk place-mats, toys and brightly colored silk-rag carpets in the basement.
➕ F11 ✉ 304 Thanon Silom ☎ 0 2235 1553 🚊 Skytrain: Sala Daeng 🚌 A/C bus 502, 504, 505

JIM THOMPSON'S THAI SILK COMPANY

The best but not the cheapest place to buy silks or a wide range of silk clothing. The quality and the variety of colors and textures is superior to most other places, and the name is international currency (➤ panel). Don't miss the excellent furnishing fabrics, both cotton and silk. There are branches in most five-star hotels and at the Emporium Shopping Complex (➤ 76).
➕ G10/11 ✉ 9 Thanon Surawong ☎ 0 2632 8100; www.jimthompson.com 🚊 Skytrain: Sala Daeng 🚌 A/C bus 502, 507

PHAHURAT MARKET
(➤ 52)

PRAYER TEXTILE GALLERY

Lovely collection of both old and new traditional textiles from northern Thailand, Laos and Cambodia, as well as some ready-made garments.
➕ G9 ✉ Corner of Siam Square and Thanon Phaya Thai ☎ 0 2251 7549 🕐 Mon–Sat 10–6 🚊 Skytrain: Siam

T. SHINAWATRA THAI SILK

Wide range of basic cottons and silks, all well priced. Also men's and women's clothing in silk, embroidered scarves, purses and other accessories. Some of the fabrics are from the factory next door.
➕ Off map at K10 ✉ 94 Soi Sukhumwit 23 ☎ 0 2633 1200 🚊 Skytrain: Asoke 🚌 A/C bus 501, 508, 511

V. P. GALLERY

A good selection of textiles and clothing made from hill tribe fabrics, as well as other objects d'art from the northern regions.
➕ E11 ✉ Rooms 423–424, River City Antiques Center, 4th Floor, 23 Trok Rongnamkaeny, Thanon Yotha ☎ 0 2237 0077 ext. 423–424 ⛴ Tha Sri Phraya pier

Tailors

A. PRIME CUSTOM TAILOR

Experienced and well-established tailor for both men and women. Very personal service and high quality work if you don't need a suit in a day.

✚ E11 ✉ Ground Floor, Shangri-La Hotel, 89 Soi Wat Suan Plu, Thanon Charoen Krung 42/1 ☎ 0 2630 6919; www.a-primetailor.com 🚇 Skytrain: Tha Saphan Taksin 🚌 A/C bus 504 ⛴ Tha Shangri-La

ART'S TAILOR

A proper tailor's shop with a very good reputation. Unlike some other tailors in the city, Art's needs two to three weeks and several fittings to make a suit, but regulars insist that it is well worth the wait.

✚ G11 ✉ 62/15–16 Thanon Thaniya, off Thanon Silom ☎ 0 2236 7966 🚇 Skytrain: Sala Daeng 🚌 A/C bus 502, 504, 505

EMBASSY TAILOR

Not the cheapest tailor in town, but certainly the suits made in this British-owned boutique are of superior quality. Embassy does both men's and women's clothes and is at its best when you allow more than 24 hours.

✚ H10 ✉ 57/5–7 Thanon Witthayu (Wireless Road), Lumphini ☎ 0 2251 2620; www.embassyfashion.com 🚇 Skytrain: Ploenchit ❓ Free pick up from your hotel

INDERS FASHION

More contemporary cut of suits for young executives, both women and men, made by expert Shanghainese tailors.

✚ J9 ✉ 2 Soi 11 Thanon Sukhumwit ☎ 0 2253 3865; www.indersfashion.com 🚇 Skytrain: Nana 🚌 A/C bus 501, 508

MISS HONG

Miss Hong is renowned among Bangkok's expats as one of the best tailors for women and children's clothing, at reasonable prices. She is very busy so call her well in advance, even from abroad for an appointment. She will then book you in and reserve the time needed to make your garment.

✚ J9 ✉ 625–26 Sukhumwit Nana Soi 3/1 ☎ 0 2253 5662/5823 🕐 Mon–Sat 9.30–6 🚇 Skytrain: Nana 🚌 A/C bus 501, 508

JULIE THAI COTTON & SILK

Renowned dressmaker in Bangkok who makes women's clothes only, including wedding and evening dresses. Chinese dresses, jackets, blouses, suits and coats.

✚ E11 ✉ 1279 Thanon Charoeng Krung ☎ 0 2337 6592; www.julie.co.th 🚇 Skytrain: Saphan Taksin ⛴ Tha Oriental pier or Tha Shangri-La

NARRY TAILOR

Voted Bangkok's "Tailor of the Year" for several years running. Good-quality work and very quick service. Phone to arrange a free pick-up.

✚ J9 ✉ 155/22 Thanon Sukhumwit Soi 11/1, near Swiss Park Hotel ☎ 0 2651 0179; mobile 01-374 0046; www.narry.com 🚇 Skytrain: Nana 🚌 A/C bus 501, 508

TAILOR-MADE CLOTHES

Bangkok tailors, mostly Thais of Indian origin, have taken over from their Hong Kong brothers. It is cheaper to have a suit made than to buy a designer's suit, but remember that you get what you pay for. Some tailors offer a package of two suits, jacket, kimono and shirts, all made in 24 hours for little over 4,300B, but the quality will be non-existent. Choose a tailor with a good reputation, choose a quality fabric and good cut and allow the tailor as much time as possible. You will need to go to the shop to choose your fabric, but fittings can usually be done in your hotel room.

Clothes

CHEAP DESIGN

The best time to do some serious shopping is during the January or summer sales when many stores offer hefty discounts. You may, however, like many Westerners have a problem with Thai sizes which are petite. You can always stock up on a wealth of accessories or take *Vogue* magazine to a good tailor.

SHOPPING MALL BOOM

The last few years have seen many smaller and a few huge shopping malls rise up above Bangkok's skyline. The best places to look for women's fashion, in particular the more expensive labels, are around Thanon Ploenchit and Thanon Sukhumwit. Amarin Plaza, on Thanon Ploenchit, houses the Sogo department store as well as many other boutiques and restaurants. Peninsula Plaza, on Thanon Ratchadamri, has a more exclusive selection of stores, including the biggest Versace outlet in Asia. The largest of all, the World Trade Center on Rajprasongi, has just about everything.

CENTRAL WORLD PLAZA

Definitely Bangkok's glitziest department store with live piano music in the background. Many international brands are available here. Take a break at the trendy Greyhound Café.
➕ H9 ✉ 1027 Thanon Ploenchit, Pratunam ☎ 0 2233 6930 🚇 Skytrain: Chit Lom

COMMON TRIBE

Minimalist clothes and shoes in natural fabrics and neutral colors (mostly black and white), plus jewelry made from fish and camel bone, glass, resin, silver and amber.
➕ J3 ✉ Section 24, Soi 2, Chatuchak Weekend Market (▶ 46) 🕐 Sat–Sun 11–6 🚇 Skytrain: Mo Chit 🚌 A/C bus 502, 503

EMPORIUM SHOPPING COMPLEX

This huge shopping center is definitely the place to be seen with all the designer brands of the moment, including Prada, MiuMiu, Shanghai Tang and Louis Vuitton, plus less expensive labels such as Jaspal and Stefanel
➕ Off map at K10 ✉ Soi Sukhumwit 24 🚇 Skytrain: Phrom Phong 🚌 A/C bus 501, 508

GAYSORN PLAZA

An exclusive shopping center that is even smarter after its recent overhaul. This is all about glittering marble floors, top designer labels and an incredibly well-heeled crowd.
➕ H9 ✉ Corner of Thanon Ploenchit and Thanon Ratchadormi 🚇 Skytrain: Chit Lom

GIRL'S TOYS

A good address for funky summer accessories by Thai designers, such as handbags, leather flip flops with exotic flowers and T-shirts.
➕ H9 ✉ Room 236, 153 Peninsula Plaza, Thanon Ratchadamri, Lumphini ☎ 0 2652 1386 🕐 Sat–Sun 11–6 🚇 Skytrain: Ratchadamri 🚌 A/C bus 504, 505

ISSUE

Interesting young Thai designer with a collection for men and women. His funky and wearable clothers are inspired by his Asian roots and by his passion for traveling, which is also apparaent from the furnishings.
➕ G9 ✉ 10/3 Pradhipat, Samsen Nai, near Siam Square ☎ 0 2279 5797 🚇 Skytrain: Siam Square 🚌 A/C bus 1, 2, 29, 141

JIM THOMPSON'S THAI SILK COMPANY

Good, top-priced silk shirts and neckties, in a wide, though conservative, range of patterns and colors, as well as jackets, pajamas and robes. Other branches are located in Isetan, at the World Trade Center, and in the Emporium Shopping Complex.
➕ G10/11 ✉ 9 Thanon Surawong ☎ 0 2235 8330 🚇 Skytrain: Sala Daeng 🚌 A/C bus 502, 507

Crafts

ASIAN MOTIFS

Stylish shop with Thai-made contemporary crafts and exquisite gifts, such as silk cushions, stationery and their very popular Chinese silk lanterns in a rainbow of colors.

✚ H9 ✉ 3rd floor, Gaysorn Plaza, Thanon Ploenchit ☎ 0 2662 6561 🚇 Skytrain: Chit Lom 🚌 A/C bus 504, 505, 515

EXOTHIQUE THAI

A huge selection of Thai crafts is available at Exothique, which has a contemporary vibe. This is a great place to stock up on celadon plates, organic spa products with Thai herbs, relaxing Thai cushions and ethnic-inspired silk clothing. Recommended!

✚ Off map at K10 ✉ 4th floor, Emporium Shopping Center (► 76) ☎ 0 2664 8000 ext. 1554 🚇 Skytrain: Phrom Phong 🚌 A/C bus 501, 502, 508

HILL TRIBE FOUNDATION

This project, supported by the royal family, offers hill-tribe crafts at reasonable prices, all the profits returning to the tribespeople living in the villages of northern Thailand.

✚ G9 ✉ Saprathum Palace 195, Thanon Phraya Thai ☎ 0 2251 9816 🕐 Mon–Fri 9–5 🚌 A/C bus 501, 502, 508

KRISHNA'S

An Asian Ali Baba's cave with crafts and beautiful objects from all over Southeast Asia, from tiny gifts to quirky furniture.

✚ J9 ✉ Sukhumvit, between Sois 9 & 11 ☎ 0 2251 6867 🚇 Skytrain: Chong Nonsi 🚌 A/C bus 502, 504, 505

NARAYANA PHAND

Huge crafts and souvenir emporium that sells just about everything you could imagine. Usually good value.

✚ H9 ✉ 127 Thanon Ratchadamri, north of Thanon Gesorn ☎ 0 2252 4670 🚇 Skytrain: Chit Lom 🚌 A/C bus 504, 505, 513

RASI SAYAM

This old wooden house is filled with a wonderful collection of fine Thai handicrafts, pottery, baskets, woodwork and textiles—some old, some very contemporary, but all carefully selected and reasonably priced.

✚ Off map at K9 ✉ 32 Soi Sukhumvit 23 ☎ 0 2258 4195 🚇 Skytrain: Sukhumvit 🚌 A/C bus 501, 508

THAI HOME INDUSTRIES

A dusty teak house full of baskets, cotton farmers' clothes, temple bells, glass lamps and, above all, the company's stylish, and much-copied, bronze and metal cutlery. They also do mail order.

✚ E11 ✉ 35 Soi Oriental ☎ 0 2234 1736 🚌 A/C bus 2 ⛴ Tha Oriental pier

SILOM VILLAGE

Within its pleasing compound of teakshop houses, this has everything—from tat to good crafts and antiques.

✚ F11 ✉ 286 Thanon Silom ☎ 0 2234 4448 🚇 Skytrain: Chong Nonsi 🚌 A/C bus 502, 504, 505

MORE ART GALLERIES

About Café and About Studio (✉ 402–8 Thanon Maitri Chit, near Hua Lamphong Station ☎ 0 2623 1742) is a very happening bar-cum-gallery showing modern art, but also stages music and Chinese opera. The Mercury Art Gallery (✉ 2nd floor, Mercury Tower, Thanon Ploenchit ☎ 0 2658 6226) and Tadu Contemporary Art (✉ Pavillion Y, Royal City Avenue, Thanon Rama IX ☎ 0 2203 0926) both exhibit and sell contemporary art by local artists. The Rotunda Gallery at the Neilson Hays Library (✉ 195 Thanon Surawongse, Silom ☎ 0 2233 1731) organizes some of the most interesting exhibitions in town.

Craft Factories

HAND-MADE BASKETS

Many general craft stores sell some of Thailand's finest baskets, but there are a few stores that specialize in them. Song Plu, in room 425 of the River City Shopping Complex, has one of the best selections of old and new baskets. A few stores on Thanon Maha Chai, near the intersection with Thanon Luang (🚇 D8/9), sell less expensive and more practical baskets, often made in the nearby prison. There are also baskets for sale at the Chatuchak Weekend Market (► 48).

BLUE AND WHITE POTTERIES

Small family-run business producing excellent-quality pottery and at a lower price than most.
🚇 Off map at B1 ✉ Surachai Nuparwan, Oum Noi, Samut Sakhon, on the way to the Rose Garden Country Resort
🚌 Regular buses from Bangkok's Southern Bus Terminal to Nakhom Pathom, but easier by taxi

BUDDHA CASTING

After spending a few days strolling around various temple compounds, you may be interested to see one of the places where Buddha images are cast.
🚇 A8 ✉ Just off Thanon Phrannok, next door to Wat Wiset Khan 🕐 Mon–Sat (just pass by to see if they are working) 🚢 Cross-river ferry from Phra Chan pier to Phrannok pier

CELADON HOUSE

As the name says, this is the place to see the largest selection of celadon ware, from the Chiang Mai factory in all shapes and colors. Check out the bargains in the back room.
🚇 K10 ✉ 8/6–8 Soi Ratchadaphisek (Soi 16), Sukhumwit ☎ 0 2229 4780
🚊 Skytrain: Asoke 🚇 Sukhumwit 🚌 A/C bus 501 508

GOLD LEAF FACTORY

Interesting crafts factory where you can watch gold being beaten into thin gold leaf. Store is opposite Wat Bowon Niwet at 321 Thanon Phra Sumen.
🚇 C8 ✉ Off Thanon Ratchadamnoen Klang, behind post office and near Democracy Monument 🚌 A/C bus 511, 512

MONKS' BOWLS

Of the three original villages, just one street remains where artisans make the black-lacquer monks' bowls from steel, wood and copper. Only a few families still produce them, and not every day, but you can always buy them from these houses. More monks' bowls and robes are on sale on Thanon Bamrung Muang near Wat Suthat and the Giant Swing (► 53).
🚇 D8 ✉ Soi Bahn Bat, off Thanon Worachak 🚌 A/C bus 508

SIAM BRONZE FACTORY

Get a glimpse of the Thai bronze-working tradition, apparently the oldest in the world, and see some of the country's most beautiful cutlery being made. The finished products are also for sale in the showroom.
🚇 E11/12 ✉ 1250 Thanon Charoen Krung (New Road) ☎ 0 2234 9436 🕐 Call for an appointment 🚊 Skytrain: Saphan Taksin 🚌 A/C bus 502, 504 🚢 Tha Oriental pier

SPIRIT HOUSES

Several open-air stores selling spirit houses (► 34, panel) and accessories in all sizes and colors.
🚇 J8 ✉ Thanon Phetburi, just past the expressway bridge 🚌 A/C bus 502

THAI SILK-WEAVING

It is sometimes possible to actually see silk-weaving taking place at Home Made Thai Silk and at the T. Shinawatra factory (► 74).

Best of the Rest

ASIA BOOKS

Offers the best selection of English-language books in the city, with many titles on Thai culture, Bangkok, Thailand and other Asian countries.

✚ H9 ✉ 2nd floor, Peninsula Plaza, 153 Thanon Ratchadamri ☎ 0 2253 9786 🚇 Skytrain: Ratchadamri 🚌 A/C bus 504, 505

CHAI LAI

Excellent silver jewelry from the hill tribes, plus old Thai jewelry. Pure ethnic chic.

✚ H9 ✉ 1st floor, Peninsula Plaza, 153 Thanon Ratchadamri ☎ 0 2252 1538 🚇 Skytrain: Ratchadamri 🚌 A/C bus 504, 505

COCOON

A wonderful shop that brings inner calm. Beautiful Danish designed contemporary Asian homeware, bed linen, jewelry and great gifts.

✚ H9 ✉ Top Floor, Gaysorn Plaza (▶ 76). corner of Thanon Gesorn and Pleonchit ☎ 0 2656 1006 🚇 Skytrain: Chit Lom 🚌 A/C bus 501, 504, 508

EMPORIUM FOOD HALL

This amazing food hall stocks most international brands and seemingly every Thai and Asian food product. Large fresh fruit and vegetable area where you can buy exotic Thai fruits and fresh herbs. Counters sell ready-made Thai desserts and delectable snacks.

✚ Off map at K10 ✉ 5th floor, The Emporium , Soi Sukhumvit 24 ☎ 0 2664 8000 🚇 Skytrain: Phrom Phong 🚌 A/C bus 501, 508

KINOKUNIYA

Bangkok's largest and best English bookstore, with a wide range of both locally printed and imported books.

✚ Off map at K10 ✉ Emporium Shopping Complex, Thanon Sukhumwit, Soi 24 ☎ 0 2664 8554 🚇 Skytrain: Phrom Phong 🚌 A/C bus 501, 508

MERMAN BOOKSHOP

This quirky bookshop is filled with rare and often our of print books on Thailand and Asia.

✚ G11 ✉ 2nd Floor, Silom Complex, 191 Thanon Silom ☎ 0 2231 3300 🚇 Skytrain: Sala Daeng

PADUNG CHIIP

This large, crowded store sells the intricate papier-mâché masks worn by classical Thai dancers, as well as masks of animals and colorful mobiles made from banana leaves. Makes good gifts.

✚ C7 ✉ Corner of Thanon Drok Mayom and Thanon Chakkaphong, just south of Thanon Khao San ☎ 0 2281 6664 🚌 A/C bus 506, 508

PROPAGANDA

Bright and cheerful place that sells funky designs with a humorous twist. In particular look out for the shark bottle opener, the colorful plastic homeware and T-shirts with absurd slogans.

✚ Off map at K10 ✉ 4th floor, Emporium ☎ 0 2644 8574 🚇 Skytrain: Phrom Phong 🚌 A/C bus 501, 508

COMPUTER HEAVEN

The Pantip Plaza (✉ 604/3 Thanon Phetchburi ☎ 0 2254 9797 🚇 Syktrain: Phaya Thai 🚌 A/C bus 505, 511, 512 is a five-story mall with floor after floor of computers and electronic gear. It is getting harder to find anything high quality much cheaper than in the US or Europe, but there are some good deals on computer peripherals and repairs can be done similarly less expensively. This is however the place to buy cheap CDs packed with new software applications. If you can't find the computer product you want here, it probably doesn't exist.

Bars

ONE NIGHT IN BANGKOK

Bangkok still has the liveliest nightlife in Asia, with much more to it than the risqué clubs in Patpong and on Soi Cowboy. Many bars have live music, usually jazz, pop, or Thai pop, and provide food as well. Thais believe life should be *sanuk*, or fun, something that becomes very clear once offices and stores have shut, and workers head off for a good meal before going on to a bar.

DRINKING LAWS

Bars are now only allowed to stay open until 1am in Bangkok and you must be 18 or over to drink in them.

HEAD IN THE CLOUDS

If you want a bar with a stunning view head up to Vertigo (➤ 57), the highest drinking venue in the world.

ABOUT CAFÉ AND ABOUT STUDIO
(➤ 77, panel)

ABSTRACT FUN PUB

Part of the lively bar scene at Chatuchak Weekend Market. This venue in particular is filled with angry young Thais bouncing to very loud live bands that play covers of Nirvana and Radiohead.
✚ J3 ✉ Sunday Plaza Soi 3, Chatuchak Weekend Market (➤ 48) ⏱ Sat–Sun noon–10pm 🚉 Skytrain: Mo Chit 🚇 Mo Chit

AD HERE THE 13TH

This tiny one shutter bar features some of the best live music in the area, with good blues bands performing, or one of the international crowd of musician friends of the owner/DJ/lead guitarist Pong, who happens to pop by for a quick jam. Lots of pictures of Henrdrix, Buddy Holly and others.
✚ C7 ✉ 13 Thanon Samsen, Banglamphu ☎ 0 9769 4613 ⏱ 6pm–midnight 🚢 Tha Phra Athit

BAMBOO BAR

A tastefully decorated and cozy bar with a barman who knows how to handle his shaker. After 10pm there are live jazz bands, often from the US.
✚ E11 ✉ Oriental Hotel, 48 Soi Oriental ☎ 0 2236 0400 ⏱ Noon–midnight 🚉 Skytrain: Saphan Taksin 🚢 Tha Oriental pier

BANGKOK BAR

One of the city's latest nightlife venues, the Bangkok Bar is slick and chic, and close to the swinging but usually seedier nightlife scene of Banglamphu. The suave bar changes into a dance house where trendy young Thais and smart backpackers strut their stuff to hiphop and techno music.
✚ C7 ✉ 149 Soi Rambutri, Thanon Chakkaphong ☎ +66 2 629-444 ⏱ 6pm–midnight 🚢 Tha Phra Athit

BAR @ 494

In a cozy corner of the lower lobby or outside in the garden, this bar continues to attract a wealthy Thai clientele with its extensive wine and champagne list as well as its selection of cigars.
✚ H9 ✉ Lower lobby, Grand Hyatt Erawan, 494 Thanon Ratchadamri ☎ 0 2254 1234 ⏱ 5pm–1am 🚉 Skytrain: Ratchadamri 🚌 A/C bus 504

THE BARBICAN

Popular British pub, sometimes with live music, but mostly DJs playing the latest tunes. Good *tapas* and other international cuisine.
✚ G11 ✉ 9/4–5 Soi Thaniya, off Thanon Silom ☎ 0 2234 3590 ⏱ 6pm–1am 🚉 Skytrain: Sala Daeng

BROWN SUGAR

Wildly popular and therefore often very crowded, with some of Bangkok's best live music every night (country, jazz or blues).
✚ H10 ✉ 231/20 Soi Sarasin, opposite Lumphini Park ☎ 0 2250 1825 ⏱ 6pm–midnight 🚉 Skytrain: Ratchadamri 🚌 A/C bus 504

CAFÉ DEMOC

A very urban café with great views on the busy square and traffic gridlock. Housed in an old government building, it has a trendy split-level bar and a loud state-of-the-art music system playing contemporary music.

✚ C8 ✉ Near Democracy Monument on Thanon Ratchadamnoen ☎ 0 2622 2571 ⏰ Tue–Sun 7pm–midnight 🚌 A/C bus 511, 512

DIPLOMAT BAR

This grand jazz bar, in the newest five-star hotel in town, is plush, over the top and decorated in quite spectacular modern Asian style with lashes of teak and bronze. Excellent nighttime jazz singer.

✚ J10 ✉ Lobby level, Conrad Hotel, All Season's Place, 87 Thanon Witthayu, Lumphini ☎ 0 2269 0999 ⏰ 11.30am–1am 🚇 Skytrain: Ploenchit

HARD ROCK CAFÉ

Friendly burger restaurant in the Hard Rock Café tradition, with yet another rock 'n' roll museum. T-shirts are less expensive in the night markets.

✚ G9 ✉ 424/3–6 Soi Siam Square 11 ☎ 0 2254 0830 ⏰ 11am–midnight 🚇 Skytrain: Siam 🚌 A/C bus 501, 508

LA LUNAR

Trendy hangout with a beautiful young crowd. Good music and a large dance floor.

✚ Off map at K10 ✉ Sukhimvit Soi 26 ☎ 0 2261 3991 ⏰ 7pm–1am 🚇 Skytrain: Thong Lo 🚌 A/C bus 501, 508

NANG NUAL RIVERSIDE PUB

A popular spot where Thais gather for drinks, accompanied with lots of delicious Thai snacks and very loud pop music. Great views of the river.

✚ D10 ✉ Drok Krai, off Thanon O-Sathorn, Chinatown ☎ 0 2233 7686 ⏰ 4pm–midnight 🚤 Tha Saphan Phut or Tha Ratchawong

THE PINNACLE

A cross between a good British pub and a gentlemen's club, and set in a large airy space with good lighting and big glass windows.

✚ Off map at G10 ✉ 10–15 Soi Sukhumvit 33 ☎ 0 2262 1936 ⏰ Mon–Sat 5pm–1am 🚇 Skytrain: Phrom Phong

SAXOPHONE

Long established bar with great acoustics and a very lively atmosphere. Daily live jazz, regae, salsa, rock or blues to put the clientele in a party mood.

✚ G7 ✉ 3/8 Victory Monument, Thanon Phaya Thai ☎ 0 2246 5472 ⏰ 6pm–midnight 🚇 Skytrain: Victory Monument

TAPAS

Lively Mediterranean-Moorish style venue that is an award-winning bar with good *tapas* and other Mediterranean snacks. The DJs turn a wide variety of music from salsa to house and everything in between. Happy hour from 6–10pm.

✚ G11 ✉ 114/17 Silom Soi 4 ☎ 0 2234 4737 ⏰ 6pm–2am 🚇 Skytrain: Sala Daeng 🚇 Silom

GAY BARS

Silom Soi 2 and 4 are the center of Bangkok's gay scene (you may need to show proof that you are over 18). Babylon Bangkok (✉ 50 Soi Nantha, off Soi Atthakanprasit, Satorn ☎ 0 2213 2108) is a gay sauna, over four floors, often mentioned as one of the Top Ten gay saunas in the world. The Kitchenette (✉ 1st Floor, Dutchess Plaza, 289 Soi 55 Thanon Sukhumvit, ThongLor ☎ 0 2381 0861) is a lesbian café with live music.

LIVE MUSIC

In the last few years the live-music scene in Bangkok has grown steadily, and there are lots of small bars packed to the rim, where live bands perform Western music. There is a concentration of these bars around Thanon Sarasin and Thanon Phrah Athit, but they are spread all over town. The best listing of musical events are in the daily *Bangkok Post* or *Nation* newspapers, or even better the website www.bangkok guide.com

Clubs & Discos

ADMISSION CHARGES

Many discos have a cover charge, which usually includes one or two drinks. These charges are often doubled on Friday and Saturday evenings, but that's when the fun is to be had (discos tend to be quite dull during weekdays). Many clubs refuse entry to men in shorts and sandals and prefer smart casual dress.

BED SUPPER CLUB

A hot spot in town is a white space capsule with an interior reminiscent of a Stanley Kubrick film. Recline on the beds while enjoying the consistently good Pacific Rim fusion food cooked by the talented American chef. Later the DJ spins laid-back dance music, but it's hard to find a space to dance.

➕ K9 ✉ Sukhumvit Soi 11, beside Global Club ☎ 0 2651 3537 🕐 8pm–midnight 💷 Admission charge 🚇 Skytrain: Nana 🚌 A/C bus 501, 508

CONCEPT CM2

Award-winning club with several entertainment zones including the Boom Room with jungle, trance, acid or drum and bass, and the Sensations karaoke. Live music every evening at 9.30 and 11.30.

➕ G9 ✉ Novotel, Soi Siam Square 6 ☎ 0 2255 6888 🕐 8pm–midnight 💷 Admission charge 🚇 Skytrain: Siam 🚌 A/C bus 501, 508

FAITH CLUB

A small two-floor club with bare concrete walls, dim lighting and lots of candles. Really heats up after midnight. The resident British DJs turn mainly good house music.

➕ Off map at K10 ✉ 96/4–5 Sukhumvit Soi 13 ☎ 0 2261 3007 🕐 6.30pm–1am 🚇 Skytrain: Asoke 🚌 A/C bus 1, 8, 11, 13

LUCIFER

A statue of the fallen angel guards the steps to this popular rave spot, and the staff wear orange uniforms and devil's horns. The mixed crowd of Thais and foreigners dance away in Bangkok's version of hell, to a wide variety of music from pop/dance through to hardcore techno and trance music.

➕ G11 ✉ 76/1–3 Patpong Soi 1, off Thanon Silom ☎ 0 2234 6902 🕐 10pm–1am 🚇 Skytrain: Sala Daeng 🚌 Sukhumvit

NARCISSUS

Glamour and glitter night-club with over-the-top art-deco interior, frequented by wealthy young Thais who like the trance and techno music.

➕ Off map at K10 ✉ 112 Sukhumvit Soi 23 ☎ 0 2261 3991 🕐 9pm–midnight 💷 Admission charge Thu–Sun 🚇 Skytrain: Asoke 🚌 Sukhumvit

ROOTS REGGAE CLUB

Small and relaxed club known for its popular DJ parties, mixed clientele and good world music. Free barbecue on Sunday nights.

➕ Off map at K10 ✉ 6/7–8 Sukhumvit Soi 26 ☎ 0 2259 7002 🕐 5pm–1am 🚇 Skytrain: Phrom Phong 🚌 A/C bus 501, 508

Q-BAR

Extremely popular bar-cum-club, with trendy *farangs* and Thais dancing to the tunes of some of the best DJs in town. New York-style hip.

➕ J9 ✉ 34 Soi Sukhumvit 11 ☎ 0 2252 3274 🕐 9pm–midnight 💷 Admission charge weekends only 🚇 Skytrain: Nana 🚌 A/C bus 501, 508

Thai Dance

The most sophisticated of the Thai dramatic arts is *khon*, which was adapted from different types of plays, including shadow play and swordplay. It was once only performed at the royal court, but now it is for everyone.

The dance invariably recounts the story of the Ramakien or the war between Rama, the righteous king and a reincarnation of the Hindu god Vishnu, and Ravana, the great demon king of Lanka. At the heart of this drama—full of passion, love and fighting—is the abduction of Rama's beloved by the evil king.

Khon performers wear spectacular costumes and sometimes masks, and their movememnts are so refined that the audience can understand the story and the moods just by watching them. The actors concentrate on their dancing, while the singing and talking is performed beside the stage. The dance is accompanied by percussion instruments and *pi phat*, a kind of wooden flute.

In addition to the venues listed below, some hotels and restaurants offer cultural shows, usually a mixture of *khon*, sword-fighting and folk dances (► 66).

CHALERMKRUNG ROYAL THEATER

Beautifully restored Thai deco building where excellent and highly sophisticated *khon* spectacles are performed. Tickets are expensive and it's an occasion to dress up.
➕ C9 ✉ 66 Thanon Charoen Krung (New Road) ☎ 0 2222 0434 🕓 Usually Tue and Thu at 8pm but schedules may vary 🚌 A/C bus 508

ERAWAN SHRINE
(► 46)

LAK MUANG
(► 34)

NATIONAL THEATER
Fine performances of classical dance and music by students of the School of Music and Dance.
➕ B7 ✉ 1 Thanon Ratchini, near the National Museum ☎ 0 2224 1342 🕓 Check with Thai Tourist Authority (☎ 0 2226 0060) or the box office 🚌 A/C bus 507, 512

PATRAVADI THEATER
Specializes in brilliant modern adaptations of classical Asian stories, integrating a wide variety of theatrical techniques and traditional Thai and Chinese music and dance.
➕ B8 ✉ Soi Wat Rakang, Thanon Arun Amarin, Thonburi ☎ 0 2412 7287 🚢 Tha Wat Rakang or Tha Chang pier

THAILAND CULTURAL CENTER
Modern theater venue for concerts by the Bangkok Symphony Orchestra, as well as drama and classical Thai dance.
➕ Off map at K5/6 ✉ Thanon Ratchadaphisek, Huai Khwang ☎ 0 2247 0028; www.thai culturalcenter.com 🕓 Check for performance dates 🚌 A/C bus 136, 137, 206

ELEPHANTS

You may well see elephants being used as "entertainment" on Bangkok's streets. Of Thailand's 4,000 or so endangered Asian elephants, around 2,000 are captive and 35 percent of these work in tourism. The Bangkok government wants to stop elephants coming into the city. Be aware of the problem and discourage the misuse of these noble animals by refusing to give money to their drivers (*mahouts*), don't take pictures of them and don't ride on them. For more information on Thailand's elephants look at www.elephanthelp.org, where you can also adopt an elephant.

Movies & Theater

THE KING AND I

Despite its popularity elsewhere, the movie *The King and I* was not appreciated in Thailand and is still banned. The movie was based on the memoirs of Anna Leonowens, an Englishwoman brought to Thailand in the 19th century by King Rama IV to educate his children (► 12). Thais insist that Ms Leonowens' memoirs were fiction, not fact, and however splendid some may find Yul Brynner, locals are insulted by his portrayal of their king.

TICKETING SERVICES

Listings of perfomances are found in the daily English-language newspapers or you can call the Cultural Information Service (☎ 0 2247 0028) for a schedule in English.
Tickets for many events can be purchased on-line on wwwthaiticketmaster.com.

MOVIES

Bangkok's movie theaters, most of which are located in shopping malls around Thanon Ploenchit and Thanon Sukhumvit, show Thai, Indian, Chinese and American movies. Shows are listed in the *Nation* and *Bangkok Post* daily papers, and in the monthly *Metro* magazine. All movies are preceded by the Thai national anthem.

Thai movies are often comedies, or karate or violent, all interlaced with intrigue and drama. Many movie theaters now show movies with English soundtracks or subtitles. To see original uncut versions, head for one of the cultural centers listed below. Bangkok also has the world's largest IMAX cinema, with 600 seats and a seven-story high screen (Panasonic IMAX Theater ✉ 1839 Thanon Phahonyothin ☎ 0 2511 5595–8).

CULTURAL CENTERS AND THEATERS

ALLIANCE FRANÇAISE

The Alliance is very active in Bangkok, offering a busy program of French movies, concerts and lectures.
➕ H11 ✉ 29 Thanon Satorn Tai ☎ 0 2670 4200; www.alliance-francaise.or.th
🚉 Skytrain: Chong Nonsi
🚌 A/C bus 505

BANGKOK PLAYHOUSE

Modern dramas are staged every weekend from Friday to Sunday. Local and visiting compnaies.
➕ Off map at K9 ✉ 284/2 New Phetburi Road, near Akkamai Intersection, near Charn Issara Tower II ☎ 0 2679 8548
🚌 A/C bus 512

BRITISH COUNCIL

The most active of the foreign cultural centers in Bangkok. Regular lectures, movies, concerts, music and dance.
➕ G9 ✉ 254 Chulalongkorn Soi 64, Siam Square, off Thanon Phaya Thai ☎ 0 2652 5480; www.britishcouncil.or.th
🕐 Check with the English-language newspapers
🚉 Skytrain: Siam 🚌 A/C bus 501, 502, 508

CHALERMKRUNG THEATER

Perfect place to see *knon* (traditional Thai masked dance drama). Restored 1930s theater.
➕ C0 ✉ ThanonCharoen Krung, near crossroads with Thanon Tripetch ☎ 0 2222 0434 🚌 A/C bus 508
🚢 Tha Saphan Phut

GOETHE INSTITUT

Limited program of films, lectures and concerts.
➕ H11 ✉ 18/1 Soi Goethe, off Thanon Satorn Tai ☎ 0 2287 0942 🕐 Telephone for program
🚉 Skytrain: Chong Nonsi
🚌 A/C bus 5

JOE LOUIS PUPPET THEATER

The only place in town to see the disappearing art of the traditional Hun Lakorn Lek Thai puppets.
➕ G–H11 ✉ Siam Lum Night Bazaar, 1875 Thanon Rama IV, Lumphini ☎ 0 2252 9683
🕐 Daily shows at 7.30pm, 9.30pm 🚉 Lumphini

Sports

GOLF

ROYAL DUSIT GOLF COURSE
Eighteeen holes.
🕂 E7 ✉ 183 Thanon
Phitsanulok, Dusit ☎ 0 2281
4329 🕑 Daily except for race
days. Hours vary, call ahead to
check

HORSE-RACING

ROYAL BANGKOK SPORTS CLUB
🕂 G9/10 ✉ 1 Thanon Henri
Dunant ☎ 0 2251 0181
🕑 Every other Sun 12.30–6
🚇 Skytrain: Ratchadamri
🚌 A/C bus 501, 504, 508

ROYAL TURF CLUB
🕂 E7 ✉ Thanon Phitsanulok,
south of Chit Lada Park ☎ 0
2280 0020 🕑 Every other Sun
12.30pm 🚌 A/C bus 503, 505
🖐 Admission fee

KITE FIGHTING
On Sanam Luang (➤ 34).

KRABI-KRABONG (SWORD FIGHTING)
Traditional martial art
using hand-held weapons
such as the Thai battle
sword, or *krabi-krabong*.
The modern version
blends weapon fighting
and Thai boxing.
Buddha Sawan Fencing
School of Thailand
(✉ 5/1 Thanon Phetkasem,
Thonburi).

MUAY THAY (THAI BOXING)
An excessive number of
injuries or deaths led to
a ban on this brutal sport
in the 1920s, but it has
returned after popular
demand in a much stricter
form, with contestants
now wearing proper gloves
and trunks. The sport is,
however, still extremely
violent: punching, kicking
with the legs, elbow
thrusts, and even taking
an opponent's head
between the legs and
kicking it with the knee.
In spite of the bloodshed,
the sport remains popular.

LUMPHINI BOXING STADIUM
🕂 H11 ✉ Thanon Rama IV,
near Lumphini Park ☎ 0 2251
4303 🕑 Tue, Fri–Sat at 6pm
🚌 A/C bus 507

RATCHADAMNOEN STADIUM
🕂 D7 ✉ Thanon
Ratchadamnoen Nok, near TAT
office ☎ 0 2281 4205
🕑 Mon, Wed, Thu at 6pm, Sun
from 5pm 🚌 A/C bus 511

T'AI CHI
In Lumphini Park (➤ 47).

TAKRAW
A local variation on
volleyball, where a rattan
ball is hit between two
teams separated by a
volleyball net. Only the
head and feet are used,
creating a fast and
spectacular game. There
are not many professional
matches but chances are
you get a glimpse of the
game when walking
through one of the
city parks.

NATIONAL STADIUM
The venue for the most
important *takraw* matches.
🕂 F10 ✉ Thanon Rama I
☎ 0 2214 0121
🕑 Check locally for dates
🚌 A/C bus 508

THAI BOXING TRAINING
Learn about Muay Thay at
Muay Thai Institute
(✉ 336/932 Prahonyothin 118
Thanon Vipravadee,
Prachatipat, Thanyaburi,
Pathum Thani ☎ 0 2992
0096/7; www.muaythai-
institute.net) specializes in
training foreigners and Thai
beginners. Instruction is given
on boxing, refereeing, training
and first aid, as well as the
history and development of
the sport. Accommodations
are available.
Fairtex Muay Thai Camp
(✉ 99/5 Moo 3, Soi
Boonthamanusorn, Theparak
Road, Banglee, Samut Prakarn
☎ 0 2757 5148;
www.fairtexbkk.com provides
one-on-one Muay Thai
training alongside professional
Muay Thai champions for
students of all nationalities
and levels.

Luxury Hotels

PRICES

Approximate prices for a double room:

Budget	under 1,500B
Mid-Range	under 3,500B
Luxury	over 3,500B

ASIAN LUXURY

There is no shortage of luxury hotels in Bangkok, and the standards of their rooms and service are among the best in the world. Travel agents in Bangkok or your home country often offer substantial discounts on room rates; check that the cost includes breakfast (American buffet or Continental) as it is usually expensive. In the low season most hotels will also reduce their rates by 25–50 percent when asked. Check the website http://bangkok-hotels-network.com (► 5).

BANGKOK MARRIOTT RESORT & SPA

A 417-room resort hotel on the west bank of the Chao Phraya, with good restaurants (► 66), a tranquil garden, and a superb swimming pool. Ideal for those with kids.
✚ Off map at C13 ✉ 257/1–3 Thanon Charoen Nakorn, near Krung Thep Bridge ☎ 0 2476 0022; fax 0 2476 1120 ⛴ Free shuttle boat from Oriental Hotel or River City Shopping Complex pier

BANYAN TREE

One of the tallest hotels in town with an excellent spa on the 27th, 51st–54th floors with great views. All 216 rooms are equipped with the latest office gadgets and there's a pool and excellent restaurants.
✚ H11 ✉ 21/100 Thanon Satorn Tai ☎ 0 2679 1200; fax 0 2679 1199; www.banyantree.com 🚉 Skytrain: Sala Daeng 🚌 A/C bus 15, 67

FOUR SEASONS BANGKOK

An impressive modern hotel in the heart of Bangkok with a grand, old-style atmosphere, imposing lobby, excellent shopping arcade and 356 sumptuous, elegant rooms, some overlooking the pool of the Royal Bangkok Sports Club.
✚ H9 ✉ 155 Thanon Ratchadamri ☎ 0 2250 1000; fax 0 2253 9195; www.fourseasons.com 🚉 Skytrain: Ratchadamri 🚌 A/C bus 504, 505

ORIENTAL HOTEL

The 350-room Oriental is a Bangkok institution (► 41).

PENINSULA

A wonderful hotel, considered one of the best in the world, with 370 fully equipped rooms, all with excellent views and large marble bathrooms with TVs. The restaurants are excellent, and there is a pool and Jacuzzi in the garden.
✚ E11 ✉ 333 Thanon Chareon Nakorn ☎ 0 2861 2888; fax 0 2861 2355; www.peninsula.com 🚉 Skytrain: Saphan Taksin, then free shuttle boat ⛴ Free shuttle boats from Oriental, River City and Shangri-La piers

SHANGRI-LA

Elegant 850-room hotel—most rooms overlook Thonburi and the river. It has two swimming pools set in gardens with ponds, shrines and a spirit house. The Krungthep Wing offers more luxury and larger rooms with balconies.
✚ E11 ✉ 89 Soi Wat Suan Plu, off Thanon Charoen Krung ☎ 0 2236 7777; fax 0 2236 8579; www.shangri-la.com 🚉 Skytrain: Saphan Taksin ⛴ Tha Shangri-La pier

SUKHOTHAI HOTEL

Remarkable hotel in the heart of the business district, designed in a contemporary Thai minimalist style. The 226 guest rooms are decorated with granite, teak and silks. Excellent restaurants (► 65, ► 71, panel).
✚ H11 ✉ 13/3 Thanon Satorn Tai ☎ 0 2287 0222; fax 2287 4980; www.sukhotai.com 🚉 Skytrain: Sala Daeng 🚌 A/C bus 505

Mid-Range Hotels

CHOM'S BOUTIQUE AND THAI KITCHEN
Small boutique hotel in a very central location on Ploenchit with 18 beautiful, air-conditioned rooms and good food.
➕ H9 ✉ 888/37–39 Thanon Ploenchit, behind Mahatun Plaza ☎ 0 2254 2070 🚇 Skytrain: Ploen Chit 🚌 A/C bus 501, 508

IBRIK RESORT HOTEL
This small 3-roomed boutique hotel has a rare riverfront location with views of the Grand Palace. Very stylish rooms with air-conditioning, private bathroom and balcony.
➕ B8 ✉ 256 Soi Wat Rakang, off Thanon Arunamrin, Bangkok-noi ☎ 0 2848 9220; fax 0 2411 1183; www.ibrikresort.com 🚢 Cross-river ferry from Tha Chang to Tha Wat Rakang

JIM'S LODGE
Quiet, pleasant hotel within easy walking distance of restaurants, Lumphini Park and the shops on Ploenchit Road. The 75 rooms all have air-conditioning, satellite TV and bathroom.
➕ J10 ✉ 125/7 Soi Ruam Rudee, off Thanon Ploenchit. Lumphini ☎ 0 2255 3100; fax 0 2253 8492; www.jimslodge.com 🚇 Skytrain: Ploenchit 🚌 A/C bus 501, 508

MANHATTAN
Modern, good-value hotel in a central location just off Sukhumwit, and with 203 spacious and tastefully decorated rooms. The service is friendly, and there is a good bar and restaurant.
➕ K9 ✉ 13 Soi Sukhumwit 15, near the Ambassador Hotel ☎ 0 2255 0166; fax 0 2255 3481; www.hotelmanhattan.com 🚇 Skytrain: Asoke 🚌 A/C bus 501, 508

LA RÉSIDENCE
Small, comfortable boutique hotel, above the All Gaengs restaurant (curries are their specialty) on Surawong. La Résidence has 23 lovely rooms with cable TV, air-conditioning and minibar.
➕ F11 ✉ 173/8–9 Thanon Surawong ☎ 0 2233 3301; fax 0 2237 9322; e-mail: residence@boxinfo.co.th 🚇 Skytrain: Chong Nonsi 🚌 A/C bus 502, 504, 505

ROYAL HOTEL
The 1950s-style Royal went through a turbulent patch during the 1991 demonstrations, when it was used as a hospital, but today it is as would-be-grand as ever. The 300 slightly aged rooms verge on pure kitsch, but there is a small pool and the Grand Palace and National Museum lie only a short walk away.
➕ C8 ✉ 2 Thanon Ratchadamnoen Klang ☎ 0 2222 9111; fax 0 2224 2083 🚌 A/C bus 511 🚢 Banglamphu

THE SWISS LODGE
Comfortable boutique hotel on a quiet street off the animated Silom Road. The 57 rooms are spotless, equipped with air-conditioning, internet and TV. Small pool and sundeck on roof terrace.
➕ G11 ✉ 3 Thanon Convent, Silom 15 ☎ 0 2233 5345; fax 0 2236 9425; www.swiss lodge.com 🚇 Skytrain: Sala Daeng 🚌 A/C bus 502, 504

A COMFORTABLE YMCA
Many travelers recommend the YMCA Collins International House (✉ 27 Thanon Satorn Tai ☎ 0 2287 1900; fax 0 2287 1966; www.ymcabangkok.com) for its central location and spotless rooms. It also boasts a pool, gym, and some good-value restaurants.

Budget Accommodations

THANON KHAO SAN

First came backpackers in search of the pleasures of the Orient, then local Thais and Chinese who saw the possibilities. Thanon Khao San and its neighborhood is now *the* place for cheap beds, low-cost eats, low-cost clothes and low-cost beer. If you're on a tight budget, this is the place to be, but arrive early in the day if you want to find a bed. One thing's for sure, wherever you stay it's going to be lively. Thanon Khao San is now also popular with young Thais as the place to go for a beer in the evening.

BUDGET WEBSITE

www.thaihotel.com offers special packages for a weekend in Bangkok as well as listings of budget hotels under 3,440B.

ANNA'S CAFÉ & BED

A boutique-style guesthouse above a popular Thai restaurant (► 64) with simple rooms each with their own private bathroom.
➕ G11 ✉ 118 Soi Saladaeng, off Thanon Silom ☎ 0 2632 0619 🚇 Skytrain: Sala Daeng 🚇 Silom

ATLANTA

Very popular old-fashioned 1950s hotel on Sukhumwit with simple, air-conditioned or fan rooms and a swimming pool in a central location. The hotel has a reputation for friendly service and appeals to families.
➕ J9–10 ✉ 78 Soi Sukhumwit 2 ☎ 0 2252 1650; fax 0 2656 8123; www.theatlantahotel.bizland.com 🚇 Skytrain: Ploenchit 🚌 A/C bus 501, 508

BAAN SABAI

Sixty rooms with fans or air-conditioning in a colonial building with more character than the usual backpacker's hotels.
➕ C7 ✉ 12 Drok Rong Mai, off Thanon Chao Fa ☎ 0 2629 1599; fax 0 2629 1595; e-mail baansabai@hotmail.com 🚌 A/C bus 506 ⛴ Tha Phra Athit pier

BANGKOK CHRISTIAN GUESTHOUSE

Lovely guesthouse with wonderful staff, 30 simple but very tidy rooms, and a great lawn with a fish pond. As the name suggests, there is a Christian atmosphere.
➕ G11 ✉ 123 Soi Sala Daeng 2, off Thanon Convent, Silom ☎ 0 2233 6303; fax 0 2237 1742; e-mail: reservations@bcgh.org

🚇 Skytrain: Sala Daeng 🚌 A/C bus 502, 504, 505

BUDDY LODGE

The smartest hotel in the street, this boutique hotel offers comfortable rooms decorated with Thai designs and incorporating a lot of wood. The very laid-back atmosphere is in tune with the backpackers haven outside.
➕ C7 ✉ 265 Thanon Khao San ☎ 0 2629 4777; www.buddylodge.com 🚌 A/C bus 506 ⛴ Tha Phra Athit pier

RIVER VIEW GUEST HOUSE

Budget hotel, with spacious rooms overlooking the Chao Phraya. A good breakfast of cereal and fresh fruit is served on the top floor.
➕ E10 ✉ 768 Soi Phanu Rangsee, Thanon Song Wat ☎ 0 2234 5429; fax 0 2237 5428 ⛴ Tha Si Phraya pier

SALATHAI DAILY MANSION

Family-run guesthouse with clean and pleasant rooms, some furnished with bamboo furniture. Shared bathrooms. Good value for money.
➕ J11 ✉ 15 Soi Saphan Khu, off Thanon Rama IV, Silom ☎ 0 2287 1436 🚌 A/C bus 507

WENDY HOUSE

Charming, friendly and in a great location near Siam Square. Simple, clean, spacious rooms with air-conditioning. Cheaper prices for longer stays.
➕ G9 ✉ 36/2 Soi Kasemsan 1, off Thanon Rama I ☎ 0 2679 1200; fax 0 2216 8053 🚇 National Stadium

BANGKOK
travel facts

ARRIVING & DEPARTING

Before you go

- Check with your doctor which vaccinations are recommended. Proof of vacination against yellow fever will be demanded when coming from a yellow fever infected country.

Customs regulations

- Licenses are required to export antiques, art objects and religious articles (► 72, panel). No more than 50,000B may be exported.

Departure/airport tax

- 30B for domestic flights and 500B for international flights.

ESSENTIAL FACTS

Opening hours

- Offices: Mon–Fri 8.30–noon, 1–4.30.
- Banks: Mon–Fri 10–4.
- Bangkok Bank and exchange counters: Mon–Sun 7am–8pm.
- Shops: Mon–Sun 10–6.30 or 7; smaller shops often stay open 12 hours a day. Most shopping centers are open daily 10am–9pm.

National holidays

- Some holidays are calculated according to the lunar calendar and vary from year to year.
- New Year (31 Dec, 1 Jan).
- Chinese New Year (early Feb).
- Maga Puja (full moon; mid-Feb).
- Chakri Day (6 Apr).
- Songkran (Thai New Year; 12–14 Apr).
- Royal Plowing Ceremony (early May).
- Coronation Day (5 May).
- Visaka Puja (full moon; May).
- Asalha Puja (full moon; Jul).

- HM Queen Sirikit's Birthday; Mother's Day (12 Aug).
- Khao Pansa (July).
- Chulalongkorn Day (23 Oct).
- Loy Krathong (early Nov).
- HM King Bhumibol's Birthday; Father's Day (5 Dec).
- Constitution Day (10 Dec).

Money matters

- Most hotels, restaurants and larger stores accept major credit cards, although some add a surcharge.
- Traveler's checks get a slightly better exchange rate than cash.
- You can withdraw Thai baht with credit cards from ATMs.

Electricity

- 220V, 50-cycle AC. Most hotels have 110V shaver outlets.

Tourist offices
Overseas offices

- Australia ✉ 2nd floor, 75 Pitt Street, Sydney, NSW 2000 ☎ (612 9247 7549; email info@thailand.net.au
- UK ✉ TAT, 3rd floor, Brook House, 98–99 Jermyn Street, London SW1Y 6EE ☎ 020 7925 2511; email info@tat-uk.demon.co.uk
- US ✉ c/o World Publications, 304 Park Avenue South, 8th floor, New York, NY 10010 ☎ 212 219 4655; email tatny@aol.com; ✉ 611 North Larchmont Boulevard, 1st floor, Los Angeles, CA 90004 ☎ 323 461 9814; email info@tatla21x.netcom.com

Main local tourist information centres (TAT)

- ✉ Counter at Bangkok International Airport ☎ 0 2504 2701 🕐 Daily 8am–midnight.
- ✉ 372 Thanon Bamrung Muang, east of the Grand Palace ☎ 0 2226 0060/0085 🕐 Daily 8.30–4.30
- ✉ 4 Thanon Rajdamnun Nok, Dusit ☎ 0 2694 1222 🕐 Daily 8.30–4.30

Student travelers

- Museums offer a 50 percent discount to holders of an

International Student Identity Card (ISIC), and you can buy discounted Skytrain passes

Etiquette

- Thais show great respect for their royal family and religious personalities, as should visitors.
- Women should not touch monks, who also cannot receive offerings directly from them.
- All Buddha images are sacred.
- A public display of anger is taboo.
- Cover arms and legs in temples.
- It is insulting to touch someone's head or back, and it is rude to point toes or the soles of feet at someone or at a Buddha image. Remove shoes upon entering a temple or a private home.
- Thais rarely shake hands, instead placing them together under their chin in a *wai*.

Women travelers

- Thailand is generally safe, but social changes have brought an end to many traditions and it pays to be aware of potential dangers, particularly when alone at night.

Places of worship

- Anglican: Christ Church
  11 Thanon Convent, between Thanon Silom and Thanon Satorn Nuea ☎ 0 2234 3634. International Church
  67 Sukhumwit Soi 19 ☎ 0 2253 2205
- Catholic: Holy Redeemer Church
  Soi Ruamruedee (off Thanon Ploenchit) ☎ 0 2253 0305
- Jewish: Jewish Association of Thailand Soi Sai Pan 2, off Sukhumwit Soi 22 ☎ 0 2258 2195; www.jewishthailand.com

Lavatories

- Most hotels and restaurants have Western-style lavatories, while *wats* and shops may have an Asian-style hole in the ground.

MEDIA & COMMUNICATIONS

Telephones

- Local calls from red or silver pay phones cost 1B for three minutes. Most hotel lobbies, restaurants and shops have public pay phones that take 5B coins.
- The Thaicard is an international prepaid phone card available at post offices, bookshops and 7-Eleven stores in values of 300B and 500B.
- From 9pm–midnight, 5am–7am there is a 20 percent discount on international calls; from midnight–5am there is 30 percent.
- All Thai phone numbers now have eight digits, so even when calling within Bangkok the "0" area code should be used.

Post offices

- The General Post Office (GPO) is at ☎ Thanon Charoen Krung (New Road), between the Oriental and Sheraton hotels Mon–Fri 8–8, Sat–Sun and holidays 8–1
- Stamps cost 20B for airmail letters and 15B for postcards to Europe, Australia and the US.

Newspapers and magazines

- Two English-language daily newspapers, the *Bangkok Post* and the *Nation*, cover Thai politics, international news and cultural events.
- The *International Herald Tribune* and the *Asian Wall Street Journal* are available on the day of publication.
- The monthly magazines *Where?* and *Metro*, available from bookshops, cover features and events in Bangkok as well as offering good listings for cultural events, nightclubs and restaurants. The weekly *BK Magazine* and monthly *Mustard* are free and have culture, restaurant and nightlife listings.

Radio and television

- Radio Thailand at 97FM has a daily English-language programme from 6am to midnight. The BBC World Service and the Voice of America can be picked up on short wave. (Check schedules before leaving home.)
- Cable TV with international channels is available at luxury hotels. For broadcast TV, check the television pages of the *Nation* or the *Bangkok Post*.

EMERGENCIES

- Bangkok is generally safe, but watch for pickpockets and bag-snatchers in crowded places, especially buses, boats and ferries.
- Leave money and documents in your hotel's safe-deposit box if possible, and never carry traveler's checks together with a list of their numbers.
- Take care of credit cards. Keep all receipts and destroy carbons.
- Beware of "bargain" gems, jewelry or other objects, which might later prove to be worthless. Also beware of getting involved in a game of Thai cards as you are sure to lose.
- Beware of taking someone to your room, or of accepting food or drink from strangers, as there have been cases of visitors being drugged and robbed.
- Thais are serious about wanting to stop drug smuggling. Border security is efficient and the maximum penalty is death.

Lost property

- If you are robbed, call the tourist police Crime Suppression Division immediately ☎ 1699 or 0 2652 1721

Medical treatment

- All listed hospitals have 24-hour emergency services, but you may need your passport and a deposit of 20,000B. Your medical insurance policy may not be accepted, although major credit cards are.
- Private hospitals: Bangkok Nursing Home ✉ 9 Thanon Convent, between Thanon Silom and Thanon Satorn Nuea ☎ 0 2233 2610; Bangkok Adventist Hospital ✉ 430 Thanon Phitsanulok ☎ 0 2281 1422
- Public hospitals: Bumrungrad HospitalHospital ✉ 33 Soi 3 Sukhumwit ☎ 0 2667 1000; Samitivej Hospital ✉ 133 Soi 49, Thanon Sukhumwit ☎ 0 2381 6728
- Contact your hotel reception first in case of a medical emergency.
- Keep all receipts for claiming on your travel insurance when home.

Medicines

- British Dispensary ✉ Near Soi 5, 109 Thanon Sukhumwit ☎ 0 2252 8056 or ✉ Corner of Soi Oriental and Thanon Charoen Krung (New Road) ☎ 0 2234 0174
- Phuket Dispensary ✉ Near Soi 21, 383 Thanon Sukhumwit ☎ 0 2252 9179
- Thai pharmacies are generally well stocked, and many drugs are available over the counter.
- Pharmacies are open daily 8am–9pm in most places, but there is no all-night service. In an emergency, contact a hospital.

Emergency phone numbers

- Ambulance ☎ 191
- Fire ☎ 195
- Police ☎ 191
- Tourist police ☎ 1155
- Tourist Assistance Center ☎ 0 2282 8129

Embassies and consulates

- Australia ✉ 37 Thanon Satorn Tai ☎ 0 2287 2680

- Canada ✉ 15th floor, Abdulrahim Building, 990 Thanon Rama IV ☎ 0 2636 0540
- France ✉ 36 Soi Rongpasi Kao (Customs House Lane), Thanon Charoen Krung (New Road) 36 ☎ 0 2287 1592; consular section
- Germany ✉ 19 Thanon Satorn Tai ☎ 0 2287 9000
- Italy ✉ 399 Thanon Nang Linchi ☎ 0 2285 4090/3
- New Zealand ✉ M Thai Tower, 14/F, All Seasons Palce, 87 Thanon Whittayu (Wireless Road) ☎ 0 2254 2530
- UK ✉ 1031 Thanon Witthayu ☎ 0 2305 8333
- USA ✉ 120–122 Thanon Witthayu (Wireless Road) ☎ 0 2205 4000

LANGUAGE

- Although English is widely spoken in hotels and restaurants, it is useful to have some Thai. It is quite difficult to get the hang of as one syllable can be pronounced in five tones, each of which will carry a different meaning. The classic example of this is the syllable *mai* which, in the different tones, can mean "new," "wood," "burned," "not?" and "not." So *Mái mài mâi mâi mǎi* means: "New wood doesn't burn, does it?" Tricky, *mâi*? Consonants are also pronounced slightly differently. Ask a local Thai to pronounce the words listed below for you in the right tone. And for taxi and *tuk tuk* drivers, notorious for misunderstanding visitors' pronunciation of addresses, ask someone to write down your destination in Thai script.

Useful phrases

hello sawat-dii khrap (man), sawat-dii kha (woman)
how are you? pen yangai?
I'm fine sabaay dii
thank you khawp khun

goodbye laa gorn
see you later phop gan mai
sorry, excuse me kor toh
what is your name? khun cheu arai?
my name is... (man) phom cheu...
my name is... (woman) diichan cheu...
(I) don't understand mai khao jai
yes chai
no mai chai
how do I get to...? pai...yung ngai?
turn right lii-o kwaa
turn left lii-o sai
straight ahead dtrong dtrong
how much? thao rai?
inexpensive thuuk
too expensive phaeng pai

Numbers

0	suun	8	paet
1	neung	9	kao
2	sawng	10	sip
3	sahm	11	sip-et
4	sii	12	sip-sawng
5	haa	20	yii-sip
6	hok	30	sahm-sip
7	jet	100	neung roy

Time

today wan nii
tomorrow phrung nii
yesterday meua waan

Glossary

bot **main chapel of a temple**
chakri **military commander**
chedi **pagoda, where relics are kept**
farang **foreigner**
hawng suam **toilet**
mae, mae nam, lak nam **river**
raan aahaa **restaurant**
reua hang yao **long-tail boat**
rim nam **river bank**
rohng raem **hotel**
rot fai **train**
rot meh, rot bat **bus**
rot yon **taxi**
sanaam bin **airport**
sathaanii **station**

93

Index

CityPack
Bangkok *Top 25*

ABOUT THE AUTHORS

Anthony Sattin is the author of several books and is a regular contributor to the *Condé Nast Traveller* and *The Sunday Times*. Sylvie Franquet is a linguist, has worked as a model, translator, and tour manager, and writes travel articles for the Belgian newspaper *De Morgen*. Together they wrote the AA Explorer guides to Egypt and the Greek Islands, as well as many other guidebooks.

WRITTEN BY AND EDITION REVISERS Anthony Sattin & Sylvie Franquet
MANAGING EDITORS Apostrophe S Limited
COVER DESIGN Tigist Getachew, Fabrizio La Rocca

A CIP catalogue record for this book is available from the British Library.

ISBN-10: 0 7495 4036 2
ISBN-13: 978 0 7495 4036 4

Published by AA Publishing (a trading name of Automobile Association Developments Limited, whose registered office is Southwood East, Apollo Rise, Farnborough, Hampshire GU14 0JW. Registered number 1878835).

© **AUTOMOBILE ASSOCIATION DEVELOPMENTS LIMITED 1996, 1998, 2000, 2003, 2005**
First published 1997. Second edition 1999. Third edition 2002. Fourth edition 2003.
Reprinted Jun 2004. Revised fifth edition 2005.

Colour separation by Keenes, Andover
Printed and bound by Hang Tai D&P Limited, Hong Kong

ACKNOWLEDGEMENTS

The Automobile Association wishes to thank the following libraries for their assistance in the preparation of this book:
Eye Ubiquitous 49t; Spectrum Colour Library 42t, 48t, 49t, 60; Stockbyte 5
The remaining photographs are held in the Association's own library (AA WORLD TRAVEL LIBRARY) and were taken by Rick Strange, with the exception of 1b, 8b, 8c, 8/9, 9t, 9r, 10t, 10c, 11t, 12t, 12c, 12/13, 13r, 14t, 14c, 15t, 15cl, 15cr, 16t, 16l, 16c, 17r, 18t, 18c, 18/19, 19t, 19c, 19r, 20tl, 21c, 22t, 24tl, 24tr, 24cr, 56 which were taken by David Henley and 9cl, 11c, 13t, 23, 24cl, 26t, 26c, 28t, 28b, 29t, 31t, 31b, 35c, 36, 37t, 37b, 41t, 41b, 43b, 46t, 49b, 50t, 50c, 53, 57, 61 which were taken by Jim Holmes.
Cover images: AA World Travel Library (Rick Strange)

A02290
Fold out map © MAIRDUMONT / Falk Verlag 2005
Transport map © TCS, Aldershot, England

TITLES IN THE CITYPACK SERIES